Anna Akhmatova

SELECTED POEMS

Edited and translated by Walter Arndt

also with

REQUIEM

Translated by Robin Kemball

and

A POEM WITHOUT A HERO

Translated and annotated by Carl R. Proffer

Cover drawing by Modigliani, 1911.

"A Poem without a Hero," Copyright 1971 by Ardis.
"Requiem," Copyright 1974 by Robin Kemball.
"20 Lyric Poems," Copyright 1974 by Ardis.

All other translations and material in Anna Akhmatova,
Selected Poems, Copyright © 1976 by Ardis,
2901 Heatherway, Ann Arbor, Michigan, 48104

Second edition, 1979.

ISBN 0-88233-180-9

It is a pleasant duty to acknowledge my debt of gratitude to Gleb Struve of Berkeley, California, not only for his great part in compiling the edition of Akhmatova's works on which this collection is based, but for his critical perusal of the English poems, to which they owe a number of valuable emendations; and to Marc, Slonim of Geneva, nephew of an important contemporary critic of Akhmatova, Iulii Aikhenvald, for sharing with me his personal memories of Akhmatova's circle and the cultural scene of St. Petersburg on the eve of World War I. Grateful recognition is also due to the Rockefeller Foundation for my appointment as a resident scholar at one of its research centers, and to my colleagues on the Committee on Research of Dartmouth College for financial support.

Author and publisher express gratitude to *Mademoiselle* magazine for the transfer of rights to three translations first published there. Several others were first published in *The New Leader.*

— *Walter Arndt*

The translator would like to take this opportunity to thank those friends who gave him the benefit of their criticism and advice, in particular Gleb Struve, Constantin Regamy, and Archbishop John (Shakhovskoy) of San Francisco. The present translation is a slightly amended version of that which originally appeared in *The Russian Review* [Vol. 33, No. 3 (July 1974), pp. 303-312].

—*Robin Kemball*

On Annotation, Bibliography, Arrangement

It was decided between translator and editor to refrain from "textologic", bibliographic, biographic, or "interpretive" annotation of the poems with respect to most such matters as the addressees of dedications and allusions, the various epigraphs and mottos, the many variant readings, the publication history. Much of this sort of information is only marginally germane to the purpose of this collection and in any case can be culled with minimal assistance from the Struve-Filippov edition identified below. The poet's personal references and allusions within and above her verse were placed there, by her own testimony, as private marks and ciphers, not as clues indispensable for "solving" her poems. Obtruding such bits of lore upon the reader would avail little without the context of a full biography and *chronique sentimentale*; in this anthology in English it would be apt to bemuse rather than enlighten.

A chronology of Akhmatova's life and letters in English, with much useful critical analysis, is found in Professor Sam N. Driver's monograph of 1972 in the Twayne Series. This book and two critical studies published by Jeanne van der Eng-Liedmeyer and/or Kees Verheul in 1971 and 1973 at Mouton's seem to make up the sum of Akhmatova criticism in English above article length. A short chronology of Akhmatova's life and works precedes the poems in this collection.

The poems, and accordingly the Table of Contents, are arranged chronologically according to publication in book form, not by date of composition or first publication, although dates of composition appear where available as subscripts to the poems. Within each book, and also where there is none, the titles of strings or cycles of poems are noted. The selections are listed by title if there is one, otherwise by the onset of the first line in English. To ease identification of the Russian originals, the page number of each item in the authoritative two-volume Struve-Filippov edition, *Works*, Interlanguage Literary Associates, 1967, 1968, is noted with the title or first line of each poem in the Table of Contents.

TABLE OF CONTENTS

On Annotation, Bibliography, Arrangement   *vi*
Introduction I: The Akhmatova Phenomenon   *xiii*
Introduction II: Rendering the Whole Poem   *xxv*
Chronicle   *xxxiii*

from EVENING
    Delusion I (Vol. I, 58)[1]   5
    Delusion II (Vol. I, 58)   5
    Delusion III (Vol. I, 59)   6
    Love vanquishes... (Vol. I, 61)   6
    Love (Vol. I, 62)   7
    In Tsarskoe Selo I (Vol. I, 62)   7
    In Tsarskoe Selo II (Vol. I, 63)   8
    In Tsarskoe Selo III (Vol. I, 63)   8
    A dark veil... (Vol. I, 64)   9
    Heart's recollection of... (Vol. I, 65)   9
    Heart to heart is never... (Vol. I, 66)   10
    The Song of the Last Encounter (Vol. I, 67-68)   11
    As if through a straw... (Vol. I, 69)   11
    Burial (Vol. I, 72-73)   12
    This place is as good... (Vol. I, 76)   13
    In a White Night (Vol. I, 77)   14

from ROSARY
    All abject, these eyes... (Vol. I, 87)   19
    I've trained myself... (Vol. I, 89-90)   19
    Don't crumple my letter... (Vol. I, 92-93)   20
    When first my dark... (Vol. I, 93-94)   20
    Evening (Vol. I, 99)   21
    Outing (Vol. I, 100)   21
    You have come, all tenderness... (Vol. I, 100)   22
    ...And no one here stood ready (Vol. I, 101)   22
    I've a certain smile... (Vol. I, 102)   23
    So I took my love out to the entry (Vol. I, 102)   24
    By smells of blooming things and dead (Vol. I, 103)   24
    In servitude you know I languish (Vol. I, 107)   24

---

[1] Except for eleven poems at the end of this collection the Russian texts used are in A. Akhmatova, *Sochineniia,* ed. G. Struve & B. Filippov. 2 volumes (1967-68). The volume and page numbers are given here in parenthesis.

The pale flag... (Vol. I, 107) 25
Ski tracks will be drily crackling (Vol. I, 109) 25
True tenderness there's no aping (Vol. I, 112) 26

from WHITE FLOCK

Weak is my voice... (Vol. I, 119) 31
You don't come to my mind... (Vol. I, 122) 31
Seclusion (Vol. I, 124-25) 32
You are hard, love... (Vol. I, 125-26) 32
First my halcyon cradle... (Vol. I, 126) 33
Kiev (Vol. I, 127) 33
Parting (Vol. I, 127) 34
The lanterns burn yellow... (Vol. I, 127-28) 34
A frosty sun... (Vol. I, 132-33) 34
Consolation (Vol. I, 135) 35
To my Love (Vol. I, 138) 36
I don't know, are you... (Vol. I, 141-42) 37
The evening light... (Vol. I, 142-43) 37
All growing closer ends... (Vol. I, 143) 38
He never did praise... (Vol. I, 147) 38
Like a bride I get... (Vol. I, 148) 39
Yet somewhere life is... (Vol. I, 149) 39
Beneath the chill roof... (Vol. I, 150) 40
When I shall be resting calmly (Vol. I, 152) 40
The immortelles are dry... (Vol. I, 154) 40
I know that you are my reward (Vol. I, 155) 41
They're only on their way... (Vol. I, 156-57) 41
All promised him to me... (Vol. I, 157) 42
Like a white stone... (Vol. I, 157-58) 42
In Memoriam, July 19, 1914 (Vol. I, 158) 43
All has been stripped away... (Vol. I, 159-60) 43
Statue in Tsarskoe Selo (Vol. I, 160) 44
Song About a Song (Vol. I, 161-62) 45
As I arrive there... (Vol. I, 163) 45
Is it my circumstances... (Vol. I, 163-64) 46
Blessing of the Lord... (Vol. I, 164) 47
Oh, there are words which... (Vol. I, 164) 47
Here, you would say... (Vol. I, 165) 47
We haven't the knack of parting... (Vol. I, 166) 48
My shadow has remained... (Vol. I, 167) 48
It is nighttime... (Vol. I, 167) 49
I liked our gatherings... (Vol. I, 167-68) 49
Spring, the mysterious, still... (Vol. I, 168) 50

from WAYSIDE HERB
    How grimly is my body... (Vol. I, 173) 55
    A string of beads... (Vol. I, 173) 55
    Earth's fame is a smoky... (Vol. I, 174) 56
    My dreams could frequent... (Vol. I, 174) 56
    Like an angel, quiet... (Vol. I, 174) 56
    Here am I, left alone to string (Vol. I, 175) 57
    I left my window naked... (Vol. I, 176) 57
    On the crest of a hard-frozen... (Vol. I, 178) 58
    The time he ultimately... (Vol. I, 178) 58
    I hear the oriole... (Vol. I, 183) 58
    The river dawdles... (Vol. I, 184) 59
    No one will listen... (Vol. I, 185) 59
    You stay new, your secrets... (Vol. I, 186) 60
    With a ringing the ice-floes pour... (Vol. I, 186) 60
    From your love with its... *(Vol. I, 187)* 61

from ANNO DOMINI
    That August, like yellow flame... (Vol. I, 194) 67
    Weathered, rusty, and gnarled... (Vol. I, 198) 68
    Phantom (Vol. I, 201) 68
    All is looted, betrayed... (Vol. I, 201) 69
    If life were just tomorrow-free... (Vol. I, 202-203) 70
    Hark, kind wanderer... (Vol. I, 203) 70
    So you thought me the standard romantic (Vol. I, 204) 71
    So we somehow contrived... (Vol. I, 205) 71
    So once again send organ voices... (Vol. I, 205-206) 72
    A cast-iron enclosure... (Vol. I, 207) 73
    Until, sunken down... (Vol. I, 208) 73
    From the shining threshold of Heaven... (Vol. I, 208-209) 74
    I augured my loved... (Vol. I, 209) 74
    The cathedral doors are... (Vol. I, 211) 75
    Tear-sodden autumn... (Vol. I, 211) 75
    Me, honor and obey?.. (Vol. I, 211-212) 76
    Far-Off Voice, I (Vol. I, 212) 76
    I have seen it, that gold-hammered... (Vol. I, 214) 77
    With earthly comforts... (Vol. I, 215) 77
    I am no kin to those... (Vol. I, 215-16) 78
    O, stop pacing... (Vol. I, 216) 78
    Breezes as of swanny rivers... (Vol. I, 217) 79
    The angel who guarded me... (Vol. I, 217) 79
    To fall sick now... (Vol. I, 219) 80
    Beyond the lake the waning... (Vol. I, 219) 80

Had you forgotten, free... (Vol. I, 220) 81
  Lot's Wife (Vol. I, 222) 81
  Here's the shore... (Vol. I, 224) 82
  It is fine here... (Vol. I, 225) 82

from BULRUSHES
  The Muse (Vol. I, 230) 87
  This is where Pushkin's exile was... (Vol. I, 231) 87
  When the bane of the moon... (Vol. I, 231) 87
  That town of mine... (Vol. I, 231-32) 88
  Rift 1 (Vol. I, 240) 89
  Rift 2 (Vol. I, 240) 89

from SEVENTH BOOK
  Secrets of the Craft
    1. Writing Verse (Vol. I, 251) 95
    2. I have no earthly use... (Vol. I, 251) 95
    3. The Muse (Vol. I, 252) 96
    4. The Poet (Vol. I, 252) 96
    7. Epigram (Vol. I, 254) 96
    10. Much awaits me yet... (Vol. I, 255) 97
  Nineteen-Forty (Vol. I, 260) 97

from WIND OF WAR and Other Poems
  Death I (Vol. I, 264) 101
  Death II (Vol. I, 265) 101
  Moon at Zenith:
    11. Refectory-like—bench and board (Vol. I, 273) 101
  Betrayal (Vol. I, 279) 102
  All souls of those I loved... (Vol. I, 281) 102
  Cinque:
    1. Like a cloud-rim's utmost... (Vol. I, 283) 103
  A Garland of Quatrains:
    Gold tarnishes in time... (Vol. I, 285) 103
    To My Verses (Vol. I, 285) 104
    And fame came sailing... (Vol. I, 286) 104
    What was mine I have ceased... (Vol. I, 287) 104
  Wildrose Blooming:
    Here, for feast-day hearts... (Vol. I, 288) 104
    1. Burnt Notebook (Vol. I, 288-89) 105
    2. Awake (Vol. I, 288-89) 105
    3. Asleep (Vol. I, 288-89) 106
    13. And the moon, lurking... (Vol. I, 295) 106

Midnight Verses:
    In Lieu of a Dedication (Vol. I, 303) 106
    2. First Warning (Vol. I, 304) 107
    3. Behind the Looking-Glass (Vol. I, 305) 107
    4. Thirteen Lines (Vol. I, 305) 108
    In Lieu of An Afterword (Vol. I, 307) 109
Poet's Death (Vol. I, 322) 109
Echo (Vol. I, 323) 109
All pledges written... (Vol. I, 323-24) 110
This is not *my* land... (Vol. I, 330) 110

from VERSES, 1907-64
    In the Wood (Vol. I, 333) 115
    Take a look at me... (Vol. I, 334) 115
    I have seen grain by hailstorms leveled... (Vol. I, 335-36) 116
    I won't talk, let out nothing... (Vol. I, 336-37) 116
    The evenings feverish... (Vol. I, 338) 117
    White Night (Vol. I, 340) 117
    Fragment from the Narrative Poem, "Russian Trianon," I, II, III (Vol. I, 341-42) 118

Uncollected Verse
    Oh, this was a bracing day... (Vol. I, 374) 123
    From "A Wreath to the Dead" (Vol. I, 376) 123
    To the Many (Vol. II, 137) 124
    Wild honey smells of open space... (Vol. II, 137-38) 125
    You have come back to me... (Vol. II, 143) 125
    For one lavender May... (Vol. II, 143) 126
    The Heiress (Vol. II, 144) 126

from SAMIZDAT[1]
    Not to have taken me along... (57) 131
    Such as I am. Would that... (52) 131
    Why did you foul my victuals... (49) 132
    All went off and... (54) 132
    You won't answer for... (54-55) 133
    No lover's lyre... (55) 133
    Like a beast gunned down... (55) 133
    Some lead off a husband... (56) 134
    Why fling at my feet... (56) 135

---

[1] The Russian texts for the poems in this section were first published in Jeanne van der Eng-Liedmeier & Kees Verheul, eds., *Tale without a Hero and Twenty-Two Poems by Akhmatova*. The Hague: Mouton, 1973.

        Beneath what rubble... (57)   135
        My head came dearly by its snowy crown... (52-53)   136

GLOSSES to the Poems (Walter Arndt)   137-139

REQUIEM
        Translated, and with notes by, Robin Kemball   141

A POEM WITHOUT A HERO
        Translated by Carl R. Proffer, with Assya Humesky   155
        Commentaries by Carl R. Proffer   187

I THE AKHMATOVA PHENOMENON

Among the remaining witnesses of the 20th century's "remarkable decade" in Russian poetry, 1912-1922[1], many still speak with animation and awe of the change of air in poetry which was heralded by *Evening,* Anna Akhmatova's first volume of verse. It was placed beyond doubt two years later by her second, *Rosary* (or *Beads,* 1914): a delicate but decisive discharge of lyric directness, authenticity of feeling, palpability of image and phrase, for which "Acmeism" was from the start as poor a tag as any.

This phenomenon ionized, as it were, the stale poetic medium left by Symbolism as it waned prematurely; and the qualities suggested above, if "Acmeist" they are, were evidently more patent in her work then, and more infectious, than was true for years of the other members of the brotherhood. They were temptation enough now—sixty years later—for trying to bring Akhmatova into English for the first time in the fullness of her form and feeling; for a dozen of her poems read in the original or in such largely form-true translations should demonstrate these properties more palpably than is ever contrived by circumlocutory forms of literary criticism practiced upon prosy travesties. As had happened in "her" city of Petersburg with the banished Pushkin's *Ruslan and Liudmila* in 1820, and in Poland two years later when Mickiewicz published his astonishing first collection and was exiled to Russia, the public sensed a change in the literary climate; the critics "pointed" and sniffed the air which had a new bite and sparkle to it.

Public response to Akhmatova, from the start until well into the Soviet era (cultural blight and official rancor smother the evidence), reached beyond the mutual admiration clubs of artists and the crushes of the black-taffeta-hairbow contingent from the highschools—although both of these elements were strongly in evidence. In its intensity, its time profile, and its kinship with an earlier, simpler poetic tradition, her impact recalls Rilke's; for Rilke's songlike clarity about this same time was quietly ruining the cult of the sacerdotal symbolist-aesthete, Stefan George (neoromanticism with a Wagnerite streak in which infinite preciosity replaced Wagner's *poshlost'*). His poetry went on, of course, to attain an unexampled and irreversible transforming effect in the twenties and beyond, intoxicating each new generation through intervening lapses of taste and sundry fads of "free form." One is also reminded of the triumphal spread, in an outbreak of *samizdat* seemingly defying all technical given data, of the young Pushkin's wrathful odes and epigrams, and his brilliant ribaldry, among the literate of all ages and walks of life in the years between 1819 and 1824. At that, Akhmatova's appeal was not abetted by any of that spice of ideological mutiny and moral freethinking which had seasoned her idol Pushkin's shockers, including even the triply camouflaged *Ruslan and Liudmila*. Not only the older Symbolists, but even those poets of high distinction who were unconnected with or remote from the mode by this time, like Innokenty Annensky (†1909) and Alexander Blok (†1921), both revered by Akhmatova, were eclipsed before their time by the Acmeist constellation. Gumilev himself, Akhmatova's erstwhile schoolmate at Tsarskoe Selo *gimnazija* (where Annensky taught Greek), and first husband (1910-18), who had lent definition to the Acmeist label by distilling often highly perceptive aesthetic manifestos, lost custom. The exotic *chic* in verse he was then mining—generations after Flaubert, Baudelaire, and Sienkiewicz, but with a he-mannerism which just scooped Hemingway—in a stylized East Africa, shocking-pink-in-tooth-and-claw, wilted all too soon. By the beginning of the War, although not unproductive as a poet, he was sliding into a sterile possessiveness toward the Acmeist movement as the other protagonists outgrew his definitions for it and, worse still, threatened to eclipse him for good. By 1920 he appears to have set himself up as a would-be Svengali of poetry for young girls of credulity and looks in the "sounding shell," his absurd studio workshop in the House of Arts for the teaching of verse-writing in four to six months.

Nor were any of the other poets of the Remarkable Decade who were Akhmatova's close coevals—Khlebnikov, Khodasevich, and her three cherished intimates in sensibility, Mandelstam, Pasternak, and Tsvetaeva[2]—taken to the public's heart with such a personal, almost romantic emotion, or recited and imitated with quite such devotional fervor between a cult and a crush. After *Rosary* was published, adding half a hundred "beads" to the similar-sized first collection, Marc Slonim and other contemporaries recollect that the young who read poetry knew hers by heart, her readings were mobbed, lovers used her verses as letters and to set the mood of their meetings and partings. Later, long after the faddish component of this outpouring had worn away, we hear—with an optional twinge of skepticism—that she was one of the very few poets truly read by factory workers and laboring women. Also, hard though this may be to credit at first, Akhmatova had virtually started a genre which had existed in the West since the high Middle Ages: she was the first Russian poet to create strings and cycles of love lyrics. Personal, unsymbolical, non-allegorical, these truly probed and obliquely reflected, almost without external detail, the whole emotional course of a relationship neither esoteric nor trite. The literary critic Leonid Grossman noted in his article "Struggle for Style" (1927) that Akhmatova had become the favorite poet of the generation whose youth fell into the turbulent second decade of our century.

Akhmatova's original and severe beauty—a contemporary aesthete's dream—and her subfusc *art nouveau* get-ups which, when seen against the foil of Gumilev, suggest a novice furloughed by a rather liberal College of Vestals into the charge of a cross-eyed ogre-professor, were at least a small element in her magic. There is one account, in particular, far from sinfully idolatrous by intent, drawn from the memory of a then fourteen-year-old eyewitness, of a program of benefit performances in 1915. After some singing and a suitably avantgardist stage happening by Meyerhold, Akhmatova followed Sologub and Blok in authors' readings of verse. Perhaps it is not fanciful to say that between the quizzical lines of description below one catches (as in the mental space between those extant pre-revolutionary snapshots, oils, sketches, and doodles by Altman, Kardovskaya, Modigliani, Annenkov which the bloated mask of her seventies cannot blot out) the strange look that can still alert the heart, as it were, touch a node of sensibility: Young Roland on his way to the dark tower, crossed with a Beardsley Salome; a young Tatar soothsayer; and an angular school-girl, surely not over thirteen, with her shyness turned inside out:

> Akhmatova, in a white dress with a then fashionable Stuart collar, was slender, beautiful, black-haired, exquisite. She was then get-

ting on for thirty[3], her fame in full flower; the fame of her *pauznik*[4], her bangs, her profile, her allure. "He will not be sending you any more letters,"[5] she recited, arms crossed over her breast, slowly and tenderly, with that musical gravity which was so captivating in her.[6]

Over half a century later, a year after her death, the veteran writer, critic, and translator, Korney Chukovsky, a close contemporary of Akhmatova's, begins his long commemorative essay on Akhmatova as follows:

> I had known Anna Andreevna Akhmatova since 1912, when at some literary evening she was brought up to me by her husband, the young poet Nikolai Stepanovich Gumilev. Thin as could be and gracefully built, resembling a shy fifteen-year-old, she took not a step away from her husband, who right there, upon our first acquaintance, called her his "pupil."
>
> This was the time of her first verse and those unusual, unexpectedly clamorous triumphs. Two or three years passed, and in her eyes, her bearing, her manner with people there had come to the fore that chief mark of her personality—sublimity. Not hauteur, not self-importance, not arrogance, but precisely sublimity: a regal gait of superb dignity, an inviolable sense of respect toward herself and her high mission as a writer.
>
> With every passing year this quality of sublimity became stronger in Akhmatova. She did not strain for this in any way, it emanated from her spontaneously. Over the entire half-century we knew each other I don't remember seeing on her face a single pleading, ingratiating, mean, or lachrymose smile. Gazing at her, one could not help recalling Nekrasov's lines: "There are women in Russian villages/ With a quiet dignity of face,/ With a fine strength in their movements,/ With the gait, with the gaze of queens."
>
> Even queuing up for petroleum or bread, even on a hard bench in a train, even in a tram-car in Tashkent, strangers sensed her "quiet dignity" and showed her special deference, although she conducted herself very simply and warmly toward everyone, without any condescension.
>
> There was another trait in her which was remarkable. She was

totally devoid of the acquisitive urge. She did not like to own things and did not try to, and parted with them with amazing ease. Like Gogol, Coleridge, and her close friend Mandelstam, she was a homeless rover and valued possessions so little that she was glad to free herself of them as of a weight. Even in her youth, the years of her brief "blossoming," she lived without cumbersome wardrobes and chests, at times even without a desk...

She did, of course, greatly treasure things of beauty and appreciated what they stood for. Antique candlesticks, oriental fabrics, engravings, ikons of old workmanship and the like now and then made their appearance in her modest life, only to vanish again after a few weeks... Even books, save for her greatest favorites, she would pass on to others after reading. Only Pushkin, the Bible, Shakespeare, and Dostoevsky were her perennial companions..."[7]

Before Akhmatova was thirty, leading poets and critics such as Briusov, Blok, Zhirmunsky had examined her work. They sought to account for some elements of her impact largely in terms of prosodic and thematic innovations, perhaps without full awareness as yet of the peculiar interaction between her set of gifts and a sea change in poetic imagination and taste that was taking place in much of Europe. And there was every excuse for this neglect of context. Not only was the European scene in poetry and the visual arts pervaded by several disparate yet overlapping and interacting trends, but each of these tended to assume different forms and names in different sections of a cosmopolitan system of so many imperfectly inter-communicating national vessels. There was bound to exist a confusing, often misleading differential, especially among individual Russian poets, and between Russian poets and their critics, as to what particular blend of foreign traditions— avant-garde, current, and earlier, German, English, French, Italian, Polish—any one of them responded to and thought the other familiar with. Morever, large poetic trends, schools, even fads, become clearly evident as such only in retrospect; in the contemporary view the personal poetic signature is as a rule writ larger.

The versatile prosody which Akhmatova developed, now stately, not lightfooted in ambiguous anapestic-dactylic beats, but seeming not just to simulate waves of natural speech, but to orchestrate emotion,[8] came from a matrix which included Blok, Vyacheslav Ivanov, Annensky, and Gumilev. The repeated anapestic onrun or ascent which is Akhmatova's favorite line-launcher is hardly encountered outside of Russia in modern metrics and is rare even elsewhere in Russian prosody before the new century. It is startling particularly when the preceding line ends in a feminine rhyme, changing the listener's interlinear metric impression, his rhythmic "intake," to a "– – – ⁄" tattoo like the opening of Beethoven's Fifth Symphony; see, e.g., the end of line 1 with the start of line 2 in "When first my dark braids...." After this flying run at the start of each line the meter often brakes intermittently, grippingly, to a pensive, brooding, or baleful iamb as halting by contrast as a spondee; an analogous design blends dactyls with trochees. These devices simulate intermittent bursts of hurried resumption, rejoinder, addition, or afterthought: "oh, and then..."; "not to mention..."; "let me add..."; "and what's more", with an unusual suggestion of rich emotional energy and rhetorical invention in reserve. With each onrun the poem, as it were, begins afresh, statements are amplified and amended, the bearings change. The non-sequiturs between observed environs and an emotion not "produced" by them but coincident and subliminally harmonizing, with which Akhmatova so often operates, harmonize perfectly with the rushing spontaneity, the aptitude for associative short-circuits, of the springboard anapests of the first foot.

Such metric novelty was much enhanced in its effect and removed from its origins by elements of tone and taste all Akhmatova's own, or most distinctively blended. These included a lightness and targetry of diction which owe much to Pushkin, who is often lovingly invoked: a fastidious economy, yet graceful languor of line learnt perhaps from the freshly rediscovered brushwork and lyric of Japan. In terms of feeling, the present collection contains touching examples of a tart girlish frivolity overlying, and suddenly giving way to, a brittle grace of emotion, exultant or desolate; notes, or better, verbal gestures of peasant piety and of an asceticism which in another might be suspect of neoromantic posturing à la early Rilke. But her austere mode of living and feeling imbued it with an authenticity which made critics call her the last poet of Orthodoxy and prompted the just-cited Chukovsky in the early twenties, with a thin sneer all too consonant with the vulgar official line of atheism, to affect surprise that she hadn't taken the veil yet. A further pervasive feature, which will perhaps be found exemplified in this anthology more strikingly than any other, is the offering of abrupt, brief, but evocative glimpses of nature or landscape, alternating with, and made subliminally relevant to, states of emotion.[9]

The flavor of young Akhmatova's initial appeal, both to the milieu of her first public and, one daresay, to some who first sample her early "songs" today, is distinctively Art Nouveau; but Art Nouveau, to say it at once, in the original sense of a revitalizing urge in aesthetics brought by the new century. Her economy of poetic line, the true ingenuousness of feeling, those clairvoyant moods of languor, grief, or caprice of a young poet were symptomatic of the great dismissal of rich, beautiful tushery (poetic Symbolism included) that was all around her. The term Art Nouveau must be understood in its contemporary connotations to do with liberation from the ornamental, lush, grossly literal which had long dominated the arts, impressionism and its triumph notwithstanding. In terms of this drive, early Art Nouveau and Akhmatova were of a kind. But Art Nouveau as painting and décor quickly calcified into *Jugendstil,* an arsenal of stale motifs, and became in a way part of what it had rebelled against, while most of the Acmeist poets remained consistent and creative. To feel the edge of the change they brought, I spend some little time below surveying the scene preceding them, choosing for illustration that domain of aesthetics which is most easily seen in the aggregate —the visual arts, and especially painting.

Whatever the differences in the timetables and itineraries of artistic trends between the Russian reader of 1912 and his present cultural heirs (who must be sought in the West, not the USSR), they share a long and continuing contact with the stuffy fluidum of epigonism, of stylization rather than style, decoration rather than creation, which smogged the second half of the nineteenth century. By way of the dry air roots of late Art Nouveau, this is enjoying a minor revival among the art-less young of all ages in Anglosaxony now. This was the Morris-down-to-Makart era, so valiantly launched, strange to think, by the high-minded back-to-Botticelli-and-home-weaving brigade, the apostles of "Thoughts towards Nature in Poetry, Literature, and the Arts"—thus the subtitle of the Pre-Raphaelite journal, *The Germ* (1850). Its tastes and manners, which one may roughly sum up as ultra-naturalist neo-romanticism, inevitably had a good deal to do also with the impulses behind literary Symbolism; whence the rapid alienation from the latter on the part of the Acmeists, especially the clearest and simplest among their talents, Akhmatova.

What happened to that powerful artistic urge of the 1840s toward the genuine and natural, comparable in a way to the noble revulsion from plastic foods and fittings and predatory industrialism in our day? A remarkable galaxy of talents in craft work, design, painting, and literature somehow found itself beshrewed by a *Zeitgeist* close to Ivan Karamazov's clammy devil of genial mediocrity, and well exemplified, say, by the flax-topped flab of ululating Rhine maidens or the nervous innocence of the sub-deb of "September Morn." This middle-class dyspepsia of spirit and taste somehow contrived to turn revival, gifted imagination, innovation, renovation, and allusive decadence all into the same thing—Kitsch. It shows how "camp" speaks to "camp" that one of the art fads in the Campbell soup-tin years (the Novecento, so to speak) consisted in admiring "Tiffany" lamps and grandma gowns, and in imitating the artifacts of a previous morass of taste in all arts but music, where the change would have been for the better. There, surrounding Akhmatova's adolescence, was the insistent fluent mediocrity of decaying Morrisdom, the accomplished mimesis of *Jugendstil* art work with its perennial limp creepers, rambling roses, hyperthyroid maidens of tile or stained glass, draped in mysteriously agitated bedsheets and labeled Spring, Summer, Autumn, Winter, which is still to be found in Vanderbilt lodges, some Canadian railway temples, and ex-Armenian cafés in the Levant. There, in fairylands forlorn, framed by unmistakable legends in uncial script, were colorful marvels for the Russian artists to see and translate into Scythian mish-mash and Church Slavonic calligraphy. There lolled, stalked, and pouted those beige innocents of the Pre-Raphaelites with their moot stares. There glossily emoted the self-conscious think and shudder pieces of neo-romantic painters of stark histrionic and decorative gifts, from Delacroix and Boecklin all the way past Ingres and the brilliant interlude of Impressionism, to such latterday story painters as J. W. Waterhouse and J. M. Strudwick (†1935!), Maurice Denis and Puvis de Chavannes; and in Germany the much more ambiguous Hans von Marees. The bottom is reached with Maxfield Parrish, that never missing link between Lord Leighton and N. C. Wyeth, whose epicene greenish couples, spending furloughs from the morgue on triple-glazed moonlit terraces, nicely combine the infantile with the degenerate and lead directly to Disney's Snow-White and the dominant mode of North-American fairy-tale illustrations (green jerklets in jerkins), Christian novelties, and garden dwarfery. In most "giftstores" and pop posteries today the eye lights with a sour shock of recognition upon billowy cumuli, a ghostly peak over a lake, somber bosks, and one or two liverish nymphlings, not naked but "undraped," which means elaborately unconscious of their displaced, but presumably equally greenish genitalia. Poor Morris...

We are dealing, then, with a movement imitative in its conception—imitative of nature and, even more, of literature—which took thirty years to decline thoroughly (ca. 1870-1900) and then contaminated some strains of the Art Nouveau which undertook to bury it. The latter has since then been selectively stylized (ca. 1900-1920) and later dusted off during interludes of necrophilia. But searching for common elements one may find, first, a weakness for neo-romantic, that is thrice-decocted, chivalry; a cult of a synthetic naivete of feeling, feigned espousal of a boyish vision of the female, combining innocence with fatality: it is over a late, further vulgarized exemplar of this type of would-be sophisticated infantilism, by the way, that we were invited by H. Humbert to shake our heads in titillated revulsion in an auto-erotic grudge-thriller of the fifties. Next, perhaps, one should note a gradual movement of taste toward the epicene, tentative, elusive (but not allusive) in human figures, a late reaction against the rosy flab of Guido Reni, Tintoretto, and Rubens, and a preparation for a new nakedness where the child-like and asthenic would usurp the privileges of innocence—decadence, in a word. Thus taste is bred down from the virile if decorative angelfolk of Botticelli by and via the Burne-Joneses, Millais', and Rossettis to grovefuls of interchangeably willowy and violet-eyed princelings aged twelve and yet eighteen, too raspberry and swollen of lip quite to fit their dewy stares or the spindly grace of their fawnlike retreats. Besides these, or Maxfield Parrish, or even a less decadent epigone like Kay Nielsen, one should in fairness look also to an honest and technically accomplished piece of Nouveau Art contemporary to the young

Akhmatova. Brilliant talents, as we noted, spent themselves in this magic maze of mannerisms—the last of them perhaps being the Arthur Rackham of the illustrations to *Ondine* or *A Midsummer Night's Dream.*

In terms and themes analogous to those of the later Pre-Raphaelites, the Russian painters and illustrators revived the legendary "Scythian," Varangian, and Kievan past; and the visual imagination of the Russian public may be presumed to have been very similarly conditioned by that neoromantic and, by 1910, Art Nouveau and Mannerist habitat. One may pick one of Rackham's angular gracile maidens, haze Rackham's elaborations of detail—eyelash and grace-lock, tendril and rosebud, dew and rue—with a dash of the Slavic earthiness and self-irony, and arrive at a visual artifact very like one of Akhmatova's lyric mood sketches at 22, as these evidently struck some of her public: "outer and inner landscape with girl," as it were. The interdisciplinary resemblance in the case of Akhmatova is superficial and misleading, as has been suggested. It spreads by association from the girl-poet's personal image to the reception of her poetry. But the portrayal of Akhmatova in those pre-War years, pictorial and memoiristic, suggests forcibly that she herself was widely seen in terms of, first, Art Nouveau, later, briefly, expressionistic or cubist fancy. It was forty years since stricken damsels first came yearning forth from Morris's saga medley, *The Earthly Paradise,* since Swinburne sang those tainted beauties for Burne-Jones and Rossetti to paint, since the Gudruns, Genovefas or Iseults out of every child's book of legends and ballads had in Russia been replaced by similar Olgas, Yaroslavnas, Svetlanas, even Liudmillas—tragic-eyed penitents prodding their sheer damask hairshirts in two places from within as they stride some desert shore. They were presciently twitted by Pushkin in his *Gabriiliuda*[10], but a hundred years later they contain the clues to that early Akhmatova image—blending the morbidly vulnerable, sensuous, and austere—which precipitated out of paintings, poetry, and gossip.

The various pat sobriquets for Akhmatova as a woman and a poet which originated then, like the "passionate nun," "the lithe gypsy," curiously miss her point. They seem less redolent of their elusive target than of those allegorical water-lily maidens of the emporium lobbies of 1912. But the 1915 portrait by O. della Voss-Kardovskaya of a seated young vestal, severely but elegantly gowned and posed, startingly beautiful, calm, and fragile in full profile, does convey an inkling of the magnetism which helped to romanticize both her poems and her relations to them as a woman. Mandelstam in his contemporary collection *Stone* saw now Phaedra, now Rachel in that gracefully portentous feminine emblem. It may now be becoming clearer why a certain amount of oversimplified art history had to percolate into these scene-setting remarks; at the risk of some sense of strain or distortion when read in either the context of Russian poetry alone, or only in the context of European painting as usually treated. It has been my intuitive conviction that both the quality of Akhmatova's visual imagination and the quality of the response to her are best approached not through antecedent poetry—despite prosodic insights available there—but through the spirit of *fin de siècle* ornate and rhetorical painting. The innovations of the *Jugendstil* period in the arts, including Acmeism, were revolts against this accomplished but meretricious theater. Its emotional force of gesture and paysage is taken into Akhmatova's verse, but she purges it of sentimentality and pose; all *intérieurs,* with their fussy preciosity of feature, fabric, and furnishing, are swept away. She goes farther than that—toward a pure dialectic of the sentient intelligence, or eloquent emotion, in poetry. Unlike other creators of the new austerity and elegance (in the modern mathematical sense), she is rarely tempted to enter any of the premier fields of honor of older poetry—the sensual-functional beauty of man and woman, animal, carved stone, any and all of nature—for its own sake, in the way of, say, Rilke with his stunning "Panther," or "Roman Fountain." Akhmatova's "Statue in Tsarskoe Selo" along with all other apparent examples of such noble snapshooting are revealed to derive their *raison d'être* wholly from the self's independent emotion waiting in the wings—often until the last stanza or line. Her abruptness, in fact, her plain gaunt phrase of the later years and often obscure transitions, were consonant with the quasi-Japanese cult of the elliptic and oblique, *poésie pure,* which was a facet of the Art Nouveau sensibility. Aleksis Rannit has much to say about this in his fine introductory article to Volume II of the canonical Struve-Filippov edition of Akhmatova's works.

"Delusion I," one of her charming young-girl-in-hammock poems, may serve to show both her affinity (or inital palatability) to Art Nouveau aesthetics, and some marked differences. Something in its mood, blended of effusiveness and languor, and in the hints of decorative sensual detail (dazzling dark-blue faience, limp morocco leather) makes manifest the nature of Akhmatova's unsought appeal to *Jugendstil* taste. But there is little posing or empty stylization in the whole of *Evening,* of which the four "Delusion" poems are part, and less in the later collections. This is single-stroke *aquarelle* sketching, fresh and swift, of delicate moods, especially vagrant states of mind drifting from small events of nature and environment to concurrent and subjectively related small events of the inner life, and back. The exact connection as a rule is logically obscure but emotionally convincing, in that it is precisely the concurrence of inner and outer events (both often in flux and the first frequently involving more than one persona) which give dual or multiple crescendos of tension to the poetic experience. In "Delusion" there is hardly any gap between perception and emotion, although it is somehow far in flavor from the simple exultation of Browning's "All's right with the world." In "As if through a straw," as often in that species of Akhmatova lyric that I would call "soul in landscape" poems, the stay-at-home emotion or thought takes a walk, as it were; an unhappy, one-sided relation of moral exploitation—"as through a straw you are drinking my soul, which tastes bitter yet goes to your head, I have no resistance left and have stopped valuing myself"—is suddenly aired. In the second stanza and the third, a step is taken into "normal" human milieu and unconcerned nature, for the sake of poetic foil, or respite perhaps, but not for a restoration of self, or pathetic fallacy; or its mirror image, a theatrical demonstration that there is no refuge in nature or the ordinary. The initial mood of dull despair persists, the poem has merely gained in empathetic force through an outdoors dimension. A different, less characteristic, inward-outward-inward turn of the poetic screen occurs in "All abject, these eyes..." There, in the "outward" stanza, the thematic association between the vernally fresh and unsteady breeze and the far-away gentleman who has the audacity to be other than sad is obtrusive; elsewhere such links are rare.

What kind of criticism, of commentary on the arts, is desirable today? For I am not saying that works of art are ineffable, that they cannot be described or paraphrased. They can be. What would criticism look like that would serve the work of art, not usurp its place?... The best criticism, and it is uncommon, is of this sort that dissolves considerations of content into those of form... Equally valuable would be acts of criticism that would supply a really accurate, sharp, loving description of the appearance of a work of art.[11]

II. RENDERING THE WHOLE POEM

A paradox has it that poetry seems to have a direct, incontrovertible, triumphantly convincing access to a truth which, when so reached, has been commonly called aesthetic. But it is a truth which poetry itself establishes by its mesmerism, and it is discernible and verifiable in no other way. A practical corollary, if paradoxes can have them, is that one is apt to accept in a successful stanza of verse elements of sentiment and modes of statement which one might not accept in prose. Why? Is it because one is more indulgent to verse ("poetry, God help us, must be a little daft," said Pushkin), pleading the restrictions placed on it by the "form" (there aren't any, since it comes about in and through its form), or because one simply takes it to be somehow less "serious," a performance which signifies nothing beyond itself? Or is it rather because the specific gravity of any utterance is higher in verse; provided the verse qualifies as such by having formal identity, even some degree of formal rigor? Its semantic charge is what it seems to "say" and then some: it says what it seems to "mean" in such a manner—elliptic, lucid, dim, portentous, memorable—that what seems manner declares itself directly as part of the semantic burden. What may be mistakenly thought of separately, as "the aesthetic effect," is of one body with whatever cognitive message the utterance might partially share with a prose statement; and the aggregate is more powerful than prose. Prose rhetoric operates in a kindred way, of course; its transitions toward poetry are probably gradual. But cumulatively they integrate into a quantum leap.

The poetic statement, then, is not just "more" moving, dense, striking, terse, beautiful, or whatever, but it is different in kind from any attempted cognitive reduction to prose. (Hence, by the way, the chilling absurdity of V. Nabokov's vivisection of *Eugene Onegin*—"yet each man kills the thing he loves"—with the scalpel of a lexicomaniacal literalism.) It is true in a sense that is both abstract and sensual; it may have truth even when what is misrepresented as its cognitive "base" in prose is perceived as untrue or trite. It convinces in its own aesthetic terms without having appeal to rational plausibility or proof. If, intellectually, the reader is irked, bored, or puzzled by an episode of the *Divine Comedy* or a passage in *Faust II*, he can be so on one level without detriment to their contextual rightness or their subliminal effect on him. The poet—naively speaking—may bore or puzzle in irrationally important, graceful, or gripping ways; and if a translation gravely fails to do the same it is useless. This is why prose texts which call themselves translations or even paraphrases of works of poetry are worse than useless; they are in effect hoaxes or swindles even when they, as is often the case, take in their own perpetrators.

Readers of Russian poetry, and sometimes the poets, have been embarrassed lately by a spate of imitation and *Nachfühlerei* by hopelessly monoglot bards of high or low estate, who were lured by a vague freemasonry of (mutually unintelligible) letters and an aura of intellectual *chic* that has been wafted about such as Voznesensky and Talleyrand-Evtushenko and, more regrettably, Brodsky and (posthumously) all the Acmeists. In our era this sort of humbug started, very mildly indeed, at the time of Louis MacNeice's BBC *Faust* and, via Auden perhaps, infected Lowell, Kunitz, and Bly, as well as some others with neither the language *nor* talent to sustain them. For the little matter of gaining access to the original verse, these poets have recourse to native Pythias or Cassandras of either sex who, all too often, their admonitions scorned, are thrown by the English Pegasus at the first ditch and depart to rend their garments in discreet seclusion. Nothing of value and kinship with the original (except perhaps to the imitator) has yet come out of such heteromorphous imitation. The case is worse with those nonchalant apostasies from rhymed metric art in favor of shapeless strings of gawky verbiage, unrelated to anything but that "contemporary idiom" which by opacity and "privacy" qualifies for the exequatur of the meterless fraternity.

A French structuralist critic some years ago in informal conversation mused about the function of literary criticism. Essentially it was, he submitted, to remove the barriers, linguistic and referential, between the writer and his audience; to add the necessary elucidating and equating discourse as economically as possible, and in a medium so congeneric and qualitatively equivalent to the work as to form in effect a true addition to it, part of its new extended substance... Then he interrupted himself and added, apparently somewhat to his own surprise, what may be reported as follows: "Of course, the sparest, most seamless, directly self-applying mode of criticism is translation—comprehensive translation. By which one means, translation of all salient aspects of form which of course embrace or constitute 'substance' or 'content,' along with all salient aspects of content, which of course include so-called 'form.' This species of criticism involves the least intermediacy, neglect, or accretion. It requires a Janus-like sensibility."

Even taking one's stand on somewhat narrower ground, one must insist that there is no other way, certainly no better way, of thoroughly knowing and decoding a poet foreign to others than by that taxing commitment to both tonal and verse-technical assimilation which is metric translation.

One longs to do this, I suspect, not so much in order to make the poet accessible as in order to test and taste him in more than one linguistic medium. In order to move him over one first has to know him rather intimately in his native medium. Exploring the poet's work at large, beyond the range of a particular translating assignment in hand, would seem to be an important preliminary.

What are the distinguishing marks of Akhmatova's handwriting in poetry—of the effective sweep of her pen and the graphics of her versification? These are intricate questions in themselves in relation to any poet of originality, but they take on a desperate edge only if one tries to verbalize them. The sensitive native soon takes these marks in; and the translator, if he has done his job, is thereby relieved of the supererogatory task of attempting the second best—generalizing and classifying by "critical" circumscription. His impulse is to naturalize the "foreign" verse. I insert this term despite its affected ring because "translate" in its colloquial blandness suppresses both the lure and the magicking labor of what some bring themselves to call "englishing," *Verdeutschen, spolszczenie,* etc. Akhmatova's register of emotions and moods, her rhythms and rhymes, and the interaction between these (which of course only exist with and by virtue of one another) have to be absorbed in the mediator's aesthetic matrix before the need for any actual lexical matching intrudes. There is no intention to suggest that the would-be recreator of Akhmatova's verse by an act of mystic absorption in her *oeuvre* attains a state of communication with her spirit and diction, whence he will speak with her tongue in another tongue. It is merely submitted that reading like this, with occasional pilot translation of tempting lines, is the best road short of metempsychosis to learning to say in English, in a given case later, what Akhmatova is saying, while also speaking as she does. It becomes easier to diagnose (or in Psychspeak, "intuit") the blend and the course of her emotions in a given passage or poem when one knows what she is able and apt to do, how cognate situations develop elsewhere; what her key words and her verbal mimicry are; how, for instance, she uses nature like a half-learnt idiom partially to encode her otherwise inexpressible inner processes; how she may later decode them by some new cipher and obtain an altered semantic freight with equivalent affective changes. One will then have encountered her generosities and engaging gaucheries, harshnesses and offhand surrenders, her hurt cynicism and proud flippancy, her numb withdrawals and arrogant flounces, her rare but terrible curses and guffaws. Only then does the single poem acquire the perspective of her entire personality as a poet.

For examples of the curious state of a poetic sensibility's being connected in parallel, living in a shunt circuit as it were, with the phenomenal world (with at best rare ironic innuendos at the pathetic fallacy), one may point to "Up the bare sky slim willowsprigs climb,/ Fanning abreast,/ My not becoming your wife that time/ Maybe was best." In "It is fine here...", nature's apparent reminder of the past is cited wrily as a condition contrary to fact in two throw-away final lines, yet it taps a poignant emotion with admirable parsimony. In "All promised him to me...", it is not an anthropopathic sky, dream, wind, waterfalls, willow shoots, or dragonflies that promise fulfillment, but the keen feeling soul that delighted in them and divines the promises of another sensibility that may comprehend all these and complement the first. The "pathos" that embraces the disparate phenomena is the poet's, not nature's.

Lastly, in order to "carry her across" with understanding, one must "learn" Akhmatova as a human being, though that status is inseparable from that of the poet as "content" is from "form." One must, I suspect, fall in love with her, a thing I have found not just easy but unavoidable. That subspecies of the Eternally Feminine that is marked by absolute integrity, an all-or-nothing temperament, a fiercely exacting, slightly outré concept of love and loyalty, found one of its purest and most enchanting specimens in the young Akhmatova. Not a great deal of dependable detail is available of the chain of tempests, teapot ones and others, that must have been her *carrière de coeur* in that first adult decade from 1909 to 1919, if her verse is any guide. Nor do we have more than disjointed and often dubious testimony to the inwardness of her relationship with her intimates among people and places. Partial exceptions are those parts of her life as a poet and friend which were lived with the Mandelstams, and which are reflected in the electrostatic pages of Nadezhda Mandelstam's recent memoirs. But from her poems, in the most extraordinary way, we know it all: no dates, almost no names, yet, in a magic-lantern show of luminous mood sketches, exactly how it all was, and how if felt, and what is now left of it.

Poem after poem hints at how she was hurt and worn by her ever-eager, ever-rebounding perfectionism. Many may be classed as discharges between two poles, one—her cool, inviolable sense of her value as a poet, which contains, if not alone constitutes, her sense of self; the other—a romantic urge for surrender of personality which dwells in her non-poetic self as formed by the epoch's decadent-exalté, Wagner-Schmagner *liebestödlich* concept of Love. The latter may well be reinforced by this artist's urge to make the best, or most tragic, of anything offered by life in its bounty. The boundless expectations, the portentous semantic charge placed on Love, on the confused, vulnerable, now runically unfathomable, now repellently trivial twosomeness, is one of the few things that nature and Art Nouveau seem to have in common.

If the long historical sine curve of literary values and modes between emotionalism and quietism, between ornate and sober forms, which my Istanbul neighbor Erich Auerbach used to pursue was duly undulating in 1909, we can make out a long, flat wave of the histrionic-declamatory ridden by Gericault, David, and Delacroix, by Wagner and the Pre-Raphaelites and many others, which crested with the Symbolists and subsided in the mannered parsimony and wan eclecticism of Art Nouveau. It is perhaps somewhere on the downslope of this subsiding wave that the young Akhmatova is located, with her emotional make-up still on the melodramatizing *Backfisch* Isolde side, her lean Acmeist technique much farther down toward what one may call the Trough of the Future. Rilke's angelic solemnity about Love, purveyed with a truly angelic gift, is very much in the air, Stefan George, the French and Russian Symbolists are still rampant; Blok, who must have read all of these (while Akhmatova read *him* but also Proust, Eliot, and Joyce), until well into the new century cultivated the poetic vision of his multiform divinity, the Holy Wisdom conjured up by Solovyov, but turning now into a Helen or Aphrodite, now into a chastely shameless Artemis. In each garb it was Love all-significant, polymorphous, wild, wooly, and as overripe as anything by the Rossettis. One may suspect that in poetic forms, in the heat content of emotions, in the swing between exoticism and sobriety, the curves were changing direction between 1903, when Blok forsook poor Sophia, and 1909, when Akhmatova began to write. But for a long while—luckily perhaps—the tense readiness for consuming emotion persisted in Anna Andreevna; and like Eugene Onegin in V. 31, her partners do not seem to have been up to it. "Girls' tragico-hysteric vapors, their swoons and tears..." are unnerving enough when not cast into powerful poems. The betrayers retreat, abashed. The sacrificial exaltations, the frozen calms (Anna Andreevna in this mood reminds one a little of a Dying Swan who is very, very angry) spend themselves more and more in a fine irony, chill or ruefully tender. And strength takes the form of a devil-may-care pride, now solemn, now *gamine*, in her real self and in her habitat: the garden where the Muse walks.

FOOTNOTES

1. When Osip Mandelstam claimed for "Acmeism" in 1922 that it had returned moral power to Russian poetry, Akhmatova had published *Evening* (1912), *Beads* (1914), *White Flock* (1917), *Wayside Herb* (1921), and *Anno Domini* (1922); Nikolai Gumilev (who in retrospect may seem Acmeism's impresario and drummer rather than indispensable contributor) had published *Pearls* (1910), *The Pyre* (1918), and *Pillar of Fire* (1921); Osip Mandelstam, *Stone* (1913) and *Tristia* (1922); and Pasternak (somewhat more remote in this period from the preceding than later) was known in poetry mainly for *A Twin in the Clouds* (1914) and *My Sister, Life* (1922).
2. In November 1961, Anna Akhmatova paid these the famous brief tribute, *Nas chetvero,* "We are four."
3. Actually, 26 or 27. W.A.
4. A current term for the metric line more often called *dol'nik*, a line of generally trisyllabic feet with three stress slots and variable anacrusis and coda. A varient of this, rhythmically suggesting two anapests combined now with an amphibrach (−/−), now an iambus, was so characteristic of Anna Akhmatova (especially in *Poem Without a Hero)* as to be called the Akhmatova line by Kornei Chukovsky.
5. See the poem "Consolation" of 1914, S-P I, 135.
6. Berberova, Nina. *Kursiv moi* (München: Wilhelm Fink, 1972), 84. In the index of personages attached to this Invaluable book, Anna Akhmatova's biographical note consists of *five* lines, mentioning her three marriages but not one of her works; followed by *fifteen* lines devoted to her third husband, Punin. Berberova's own entry lists thirteen of her works.
7. Kornei Chukovsky, "Anna Akhmatova," in *Sobranie soch. v 6 tomakh* (M. 1967), 725-26 *passim*. Translated by Walter Arndt.
8. N. V. Nedobrovo begins his sensitive essay of April 1914 (endorsed by Anna Akhmatova years later as the piece of criticism she considered closest to the mark), by analyzing the eight lines of "True tenderness there's no aping": "The language is simple and colloquial—perhaps nearly to the point where it ceases being poetry? But on rereading we notice that if people were to converse like this, it would be enough to exchange two or three quatrains to have exhausted the common run of human relationships and be left in a realm of silence..." After demonstrating interaction of metric and lexical values for a page or two, Nedobrovo continues: "Turning our attention to the poem's structure, we are inevitably persuaded again of the freedom and potency of Akhmatova's poetic language. An eight-line poem of two differently rhymed quatrains here falls into three syntactic structures, the first taking up two lines, the second four, the third again two. Thus the second syntactic structure, closely linked by rhyme with the first and third, links the two (stanzaic quatrains) by its own (syntactic, not prosodic) unity, and this link is flexible, though strong. I remarked earlier, by way of the dramatic effect of introducing the second "No use," that the change of rhyme scheme and elsewhere is perceived by the reader and has powerful effect.... The device described, i.e., a complete syntactical structure bridging two rhyme schemes, so that sentences bend stanzas in the

middle and finally round them off as stanzas do sentences, is extremely characteristic of Akhmatova; by this means she achieves a peculiar flexibility and subtlety of line, for lines so made take on a serpentine quality. At times Anna Akhmatova uses this device with the consummate ease of a virtuoso."

9. In the fourth section of his article quoted above Nedobrovo makes some analytic remarks apposite here: "In the poems examined, the highly-strung intensity of the feelings and the unerring precision and clarity of their expression are overwhelming and need no laboring. Here lies Akhmatova's strength. What pleasure to find that, far from being irked by alleged inexpressibility in the poet's work, one reads turns of phrases which seem to have been taken straight from folk tradition.

For ages man has worn himself out struggling with the difficulty of expressing his inner life in words; yoked by silence, the spirit's growth is sluggish. There are poets who, like Hermes of old, teach man to speak, to release his inner force to work its will freely, and those who have hearts to feel will cherish their memory.

The emotional intensity in Akhmatova's diction at times generates such light and heat as to fuse man's inner world with the outer. Only when this happens do we find the outer world depicted in Akhmatova's verse; hence her pictures of that world are not soberly naturalistic, but stabbed with shafts of feeling as if seen with the eyes of a drowning man:

> It grows light. And over the smithy
> Rises smoke
> Oh, you couldn't once more be with me
> Sad in my yoke.

Or the continuation of the poem about the pleading eyes:

> I walk down the path—on its margin
> Lie timbers in stacks of grey—
> To fields a breeze is at large in
> Like the spiring, uneven and gay.

Sometimes her lyrical intensity constrains Akhmatova to do no more than hint at the suffering which is seeking expression in nature; and yet through her description one senses the heartbeat of feeling:

> In servitude you know I languish,
> For leave to die I plead with God,
> But always, to the edge of anguish,
> I see the Tver-land's grudging sod.
>
> A weathered well with hauling-crane,
> Above it clouds, like vapor leaking,
> Out in the fields the stile-gate creaking,
> And heartache—in the fragrant grain.
>
> Those unspectacular expanses
> Where even winds dare not alarm,
> And those evaluating glances
> Of countrywomen tanned and calm.

That low-voiced wind, though, brings tears to one's eyes."

10. Lines 13-16: "Sixteen of age, pliant of soul and modest,/ Raven her brow, the maiden mounds below/ Asway against the tautened linen bodice,/ A lovesome foot, her teeth a pearly row..."

11. Susan Sontag, *Against Interpretation and Other Essays* (New York: 1969).

CHRONICLE

1889	Anna Andreevna (Gorenko) born in a suburb of Odessa June 11. The Orthodox cross on her grave, oddly, shows June 23 (old calendar) for her birth date and March 5 (new calendar) for her death. A number of contemporaries accept 1888 as the year of her birth.
1889-1907	Childhood and adolescence near St. Petersburg, mainly Tsarskoe Selo, the Imperial residence, where she attends the city lycée; summers spent on the Black Sea coast. Her father early abandons the family. She begins to write verse at eleven, later adopts as poetic mentors first I. Annensky, then N. Gumilev. Last lyceum year and brief study of law at Kiev 1906-07, then return to Petersburg and eventually Tsarskoe Selo.
1907	Some of AA's verse placed in Gumilev's Paris journal *Sirius*. AA herself in a letter of May, 1962, counts the spring of 1911 as her publishing debut.
1910-1913	The expansive years: Spring '10 spent in Paris; first of very few sojourns abroad. Marriage '10 to Gumilev, return to Paris in '11. Lively part in Petersburg literary life. Among contacts with intellectuals and artists abroad, the closest is with Amedeo Modigliani (in Paris since '06), which produces over a dozen portrait sketches of AA. Journeying in the Po valley and beyond deepens an early sense of kinship with the classical world, Dante, and Romance letters. First volume of verse, *Evening*, published in a minute printing in '12. Only child, Lev, born in '12. She joins Gumilev and Mandelstam as a member of the Acmeist Poets' Guild. By '13, noticeable change sets in in the character of AA's poetry—moods of reverie, languor, occasionaly histrionic touches giving way to starker more poignant effects. The war merely deepens this development.
1913-1914	Publication of second book of verse, *Beads* (or *Rosary*), which went through several editions and launched the Akhmatova "craze." First long poem, "By the Sea's

	Edge," substantially completed. Outbreak of World War; Gumilev enlists. AA continues to spend the season at Petersburg, summers writing at her mother-in-law's estate, Slepnevo.
1917	Third book of verse, *White Flock*, published just before the Bolshevik coup. Gumilev returns.
1918	AA divorced from Gumilev; keeps aloof for some years from literary gatherings, working for publishing firms and the College of Agriculture.
1921	Publication of "By the Sea's Edge" and a sizeable fourth book of verse, *Anno Domini MCMXXI*, which incorporated the slender collection issued earlier that year under the title *Wayside Herb* (usually translated literally and misleadingly as "Plaintain"). AA reads from her latest volume. In August she attends Alexander Blok's obsequies. Soon after, Gumilev, seized on a charge of counter-revolutionary conspiracy, is executed. Like Pasternak in this period, but with surer insight and firmer resolve, AA turns her back on the delusive egalitarian and utopian trappings of the dictatorship and withdraws further from public life.
1923	New edition of *Anno Domini* (without the year cipher), containing some additional poems. From now until 1940, except for some verse translations and two of a number of pioneering Pushkin studies, AA remains unpublished.
1925	AA's first "expulsion" (disclosed by her in 1965) from Soviet literature by an unpublished resolution of the Party's central committee, forbidding publication of her verse. Probably partly in consequence of this ban, she appears to have written only about a dozen poems in some 15 years. Critical studies of her work, however, do appear in this period.
1934	In the course of the rising Stalinist terror, AA's 20-year-old son, Lev Gumilev, is arrested, but soon released. Jailed again in 1937, he is released only for war service in 1941.

1940	Several poems published in magazines. Later, a partially new collection, *From Six Books*, anthologizes (with conspicuous omission of items containing religious motifs or similes) her earlier five volumes and adds a sixth cycle, called here *Willow Tree*, in a later anthology *Bulrushes (or Reeds)*. Favorable reception, interview published in *Literaturnaja Gazeta,* but edition apparently suppressed the next year. Writing of poetry resumed.
1941	AA experience the siege and defense of Leningrad until evacuated the next spring to Moscow, then Tashkent in Uzbekistan, where she remains until 1944. Asian nature and folk culture color much of her poetry. She shares an Uzbek cabin with her lifelong friend, Nadezhda, the martyred Osip Mandelstam's widow, and resumes and active role in the company of other evacuated writers and artists, apparently to the rising displeasure of the cultural guardians.
1942-1945	Recognition and publication in journals (once including even *Pravda*) continues, mostly of the more declamatory patriotic verse. A slim volume of these and some earlier pieces appears in 1943. Preparation of an edition of AA's collected works begins.
1946	Stalinist repression of literature regains full force after wartime truce. Party rebukes journals hospitable to AA. Stalin's ideological inquisitor, Zhdanov (today the eponymic patron of Leningrad University), viciously denounces Zoshchenko and AA; this brands them as free game to lower Party hacks. Expulsion of AA from Writer's Union, equivalent to ban on publication. The ready printing of AA's collected works is destroyed; only one surviving copy has ever come to light.
1949-1950	Lev Gumilev once more arrested, probably as part of the persecution of his mother, and sentenced to fifteen years in the Gulag Archipelago; released only four years after Stalin's demise. Soviet "Peace" propaganda, prompted by nuclear inferiority, at its height; AA published some poems of similar tenor in a vain effort to help her son.

1951-1956	Until the post-Stalin "thaw," AA publishes only verse translations from Asiatic languages; she deprecates the value of this work in the absence of bilingual competence.
1956-1961	AA is able to resume periodical and press publication of own verse. In 1958 her work is excerpted for an anthology, and her first new collection in 35 years, *Poems,* is issued, made up to only ca. 30% of her best, pre-1921, work, but signalling that it might soon be safe to know her again. Another, larger volume, in 1961, contains a more balanced collection spanning the period 1909-1960; but her integration into Soviet (as distinct from Russian) culture can never be more than partial, bitter, and secretly disdainful. *A Poem Without a Hero* and *Requiem,* the two cycles of her late, powerful, and most outspokenly humanistic poetry, where the marks of an epoch and the events of history are conjured up by the shorthand of personal memory and resurgent emotion, are first published in New York (1960) and Munich (1963), respectively.
1964	AA restored to membership of the Writer's Union and accorded honorific "election" to its executive committee. Allowed to go abroad, first time in half a century, to receive the Etna-Taormina Poetry Prize in Catania—an award acknowledged by her in Italian and peculiarly welcome in view of her lifelong intimacy with Dante and Italian letters.
1965	Granted a passport a second time in June, she travels to England and France, seeing old and new friends. Honorary D. Litt. awarded her at Oxford. Her fullest collection of verse yet appears under the title *The Course of Time,* in which the last and largest portion, ca. 150 poems, some early, most late, figure as *Seventh Book.*
1966	A. I. Pavlovsky's *Anna Akhmatova* is published, the first book-length critical study of her in Russia since the early twenties. AA dies on March 5; obsequies by Russian Orthodox rites at Komarovo, the village near Leningrad where she had lived since the early 'sixties.

from EVENING

Delusion I

M. A. Zmunchilla

The sun of spring; this morning's drunk with it,
And keener is the terrace roses' scent,
The sky outglitters cobalt glazes, blinding.
A copybook in limp morocco binding:
I read there elegiac ardors spent
In verse for my grandmother's benefit.

I see the path right to the gate, and whitely
The posts stand out against the emerald lawn.
The heart loves with a sweet and reckless verve!
It dotes on beds of flowers empetalled brightly,
The crow upon the wing with raucous caw,
And, down the dwindling path, the archway's curve.

⁂

Delusion II

Sultry breezes wander, parching,
By the sun one's arms are seared,
Over me a bluely arching
Cupola of glass is reared.

Immortelles are drily fragrant
In my half unbraided hair.
Of the rugged fir-stump, vagrant
Ants have made a thoroughfare.

There the pond is silvered slowly,
Living now is freshly light...
Whom today will slumber show me
In my hammock netting bright?

1910, Kiev

Delusion III

Dark-blue earth. The winds becalmed above it,
Glaring light is summoning me home.
Who is there, I wonder...my beloved?
Could it be my bridegroom come?..

On the terrace, well-known profile; waiting,
One can hear them talk in quiet tone.
Oh, a lassitude so captivating
To this day I have not known.

Poplars rustled, plaintively expiring,
Tender fantasies had called on them,
Heaven is the hue of burnished iron,
And the stars opaque and dim.

Of white stock a posy I have ready.
Secret flame for him is in their calm
Who in taking them from hands unsteady
Should encounter a warm palm.

Tsarskoe Selo, 1910

*

Love vanquishes craftily, weaving
Enchantments artless and fey.
So lately, it's past believing,
You hadn't turned doleful and gray.

And when she would smile, wherever,
In the fields, in your house, under trees,
It did not occur to you ever
But that you were free, and at ease.

Serene you were, deep in thrall
To her and her poison brew.

The stars were so big, after all,
And the herbs, after all, smelled so new
That in autumn grew.

Tsarskoe Selo, 1911

*

Love

Now by the heart, furled still
Like a snakelet, its magic brewing,
Now on the white of the sill
Whole days as a dovelet cooing,

Now a glint in the hoarfrost's glaring,
Now an edge to the stock's slow scent,
But surely and secretly bearing
Away from delight and content.

So sweetly it melts its distresses
In the violin's suppliant moan,
And it frightens one when one guesses
Its lurk in a smile yet unknown.

Tsarskoe Selo, 1911

*

In Tsarskoe Selo, I

Down the avenue horses are trotted.
Manes parted like waves combed in two.
O you witching town, riddle-emplotted,
I am sad to have fallen for you.

It is strange to recall: I was writhing,
In a coma gasped out for the end.

And here look at me, frolicking blithely
Like my cockatoo, roseate friend.

No foreboding of hurt has me run-down,
You may look in my eyes any day.
I dislike just the hour before sundown,
The sea-breeze, and the words "go away."

1911

*

In Tsarskoe Selo II

..My marble counterpart is there,
Flung prostrate in the maple clearing;
He gave the lake his visage fair,
The rustling greenery his hearing.

And rains will lave in lucent spate
His blood-encrusted wound...O you,
O frigid one, o white one, wait,
I will become marmoreal too.

1911

*

In Tsarskoe Selo III

Down the tree-rows a swarthy youngster
Roamed the banks of the lake and pined,
And a century now amongst us
Have his whispering steps been enshrined.

The firs have spikily nested
In needlework each low tree...

Here his three-cornered hat once rested,
And a dog-eared tome of Parny.

Tsarskoe Selo, 1911

*

A dark veil, underneath she was twisting
Her hands..."Why so shaken today?"
"I have sent him all sodden and listing
With an excess of bitter dismay.

I can't bear it! He went from me, quailing,
With his lips all distorted and grim...
I flew down, never touching the railing,
And I raced to the gate after him.

And I gasped: "All that's happened here lately,
Forget; if you go, I am dead!"
His smile was so spectral and stately,
"Go in out of the wind," he said.

Kiev, 1911

*

Heart's recollection of sun is failing,
Grass turning sere,
Wind taking earliest snow-lace sailing,
Ever so sheer.

Water in narrow canals stopped lapping,
Turning to glass.
Here not a thing ever stands to happen,
Nothing, alas!

Up the bare sky slim willow-sprigs climb,
Fanning abreast.
My not becoming your wife that time
Maybe was best.

Heart's recollection of sun is fading
What—gone the light?
Maybe so. Winter may come invading
Tonight.

Kiev, 1911

*

Heart to heart is never riveted,
If you want to—spread your sail.
Lots of luck, they say, hangs pivoted
For the heartloose on the scale.

I'm not weeping, I don't cry and shout,
Luck and I just don't agree.
No, don't kiss me, I'm all tired out—
Death will come and nuzzle me.

Spent are days of jagged agony,
Just as winter's white unfroze.
Why would you, God knows, why should you be
Better than the one I chose?

1911

The Song of the Last Encounter

How past mending my heart was frozen,
Yet the tread of my feet was light.
For my left I found I had chosen
The glove that belonged on the right.

It appeared that the stairs were many,
Yet I knew there were only three!
In the maples, autumnal, uncanny,
Bade a whisper: "Come die with me!

I'm betrayed by my destiny, snarling,
Inconstant, lugubrious shrew."
And I answered it: "Darling, darling!
So am I—I will die with you..."

Thus the song of the last encounter.
I glanced up at the dark house, where
Just the bedroom candles were mounting
A dispassionate yellow glare.

1911, Tsarskoe Selo

*

As if through a straw, you are drinking
My soul. It tastes bitter and heady.
I shan't halt the ordeal by shrinking,
Oh, I've weeks' worth of quiet ready.

Let me know when you're done. It's no bother
For my soul to have drained away.
I'll go off just a little farther
To watch where the children play.

On the gooseberries hangs a new cover
Of bloom. They haul bricks by the lean-to.

Who *are* you: my brother? my lover?
I can't think, and there is no need to.

How unsheltered, how bright it is; surely
To the weary comes respite this way...
And the people who pass think obscurely:
She's been widowed—no more than a day.

Tsarskoe Selo, 1911

*

Burial

A grave site, I need one badly,
Don't you know one, as bright as can be?
In the fields it's so cold, and sadly
Stare the pebble banks by the sea.

She is used to the quiet around us,
And she likes the light of the sun.
I'll build her a cell, as sound as
Our house, on this plot for one.

There'll be a door between the windows,
An ikon lamp within,
It'll look like a heart of cinders
Aglow with a crimson sheen.

She was ill, you must know, and straying
In another, a heavenly land,
But a monk upbraided her, saying:
"No, from Paradise sinners are banned."

She whitened with pain and only
Could breathe: "I am going with you!"
Here we are, then, adrift and lonely
At the verge of a surf of blue.

Tsarskoe Selo, 1911

This place is as good as any to mope!
I've come here at a loose end.
The windmill slumbers on the slope.
Here are years of silence to spend.

Over a wilted bindweed frond
A bee does its floating glide;
I call the watermaid at the pond,
But the watermaid has died.

The wide pond is shrunken shallow,
Filmed over with slimy brown,
A slight moon rides in pallor
The shivering aspen crown.

I find it all new and heady,
Moist flows the poplar scent.
I am still, earth, silently ready
To turn into thee again.

Tsarskoe Selo, 1911

In a White Night

I left the door unfastened,
I did not strike a light,
I never, though exhausted,
Lay down, you know, that night.

To watch the pine-fronds blurring
The sunset's glimmering spoors,
Gasp at some voice's burring
In passing just like yours,

And know this is the curtain,
And life, the scourge and rack!
Oh, I had known for certain
That you were coming back.

Tsarskoe Selo, 1911

from ROSARY

All abject, these eyes implore me
To spare them—but how, on what ground,
When they utter that name before me
Of the brisk and tuneful sound.

I walk down the path—on its margin
Lie timbers in stacks of gray—
To fields a breeze is at large in
Like the spring, uneven and gay.

The langorous heart in secret
Hears word of one far from here.
I know he's alive, he's breathing,
He dares to feel other than drear.

1912

*

I've trained myself to simple, prudent living,
I scan the sky and pray to God for calm
And go on rambling walks before the evening
To set at rest unwarranted alarm.

The burdocks' rustle carries up the slope,
Here nod the rowan's orange-yellow clusters,
While I address in verse of sprightly hope
Ephemeral life, ephemeral and lustrous.

Then I come back, my fluffy cat conferring
A lick and louder purring for my sake;
An oriflamme of dazzling light is stirring
Atop the sawmill turret by the lake.

Once in a while the stork will tear asunder
The stillness as he lands with caw and veer.
If you came knocking at my door, I wonder—
It seems to me I might not even hear.

1912

Don't crumple my letter, dearest,
Read it through to the end, my sweet.
I got tired of being the merest
Incognita down your street.

I am yours, your beloved—no winces,
No glaring from narrowed eye.
Not a shepherdess, not a princess,
Nor a nun any more am I.

In this workaday dress, all faded,
These down-at-heel shoes I came...
But the burning embrace, the shaded
Awe-widened eyes are the same.

Don't crumple my letter, dearest,
Don't weep for a cherished lie,
In your shabby old kit-bag, nearest
The bottom, there lay it by.

1912

*

When first my dark braids were diluted
With a sinuous silvery skein,
You only, o nightingale muted,
Would have known the abasement and pain.

You who filter the far through your hearing
And, fluffed-up—not a breath, not a sound—
Stare transfixed at the brush-willow clearing
Where the strains of another resound.

For so lately as yet, so lately
All about you the poplars were stilled,
As ineffably gaily and greatly
Your poison notes fluted and trilled.

1911

Evening

Chords in the park intoned emotion
Of grief impossible to state.
The ice-cupped oysters on the plate
Smelled fresh and keenly of the ocean.

"My love is constant," so he told me,
And laid his hand upon my dress.
How far they feel from a caress,
These hands that touch but do not hold me.

Thus one may stroke a cat, a bird
Look some trim circus-rider over,
These eyes remain amused but sober,
By gauzy golden lashes blurred.

And fiddles filter taunting bars
Through swathes of smoke that trail and hover:
"Down on your knees and thank your stars—
Alone, the first time, with your lover."

March, 1913

*

Outing

The cab-roof brushed against my plume.
I glanced into his eyes.
My heart ached, the cause behind its gloom
Unable itself to surmise.

Tonight is windless and locked in grief
Beneath the heavens' clouded dome,
And the Bois is traced in faint relief
Like an aquatint in an antique tome.

A petrol-and-lilac-scented breeze,
A truce where alert still lingers...
There, he again has touched my knees
With almost unshaking fingers.

May, 1913

*

You have come, all tenderness and meekness,
To give solace to me, dear...
While I cannot lift my head for weakness,
And the window's closely gridded here.

You set foot into this place expecting
I'd be dead, and brought an artless wreath.
How you stab the heart with smiles reflecting
Your caress, your mockery and grief.

Where's my agony unto perdition?
Stay a little longer with me here,
And I'll beg the Lord to grant remission
To yourself and all whom you hold dear.

Petersburg
May, 1913

*

...And no one here stood ready
To meet me with a torch.
By lunar gleams, unsteady,
I crossed the silent porch.

And with a smile that faltered
Beneath the lamp's green cone:

"Your voice is strangely altered,"
He whispers, "Cendrillon..."

The fire has settled deeper;
The cricket's chirpings wane.
Oh! someone's kept my slipper
To know me by again;

And gave me three carnations,
Not looking in my face.
Dear tokens, confirmations —
Where is a hiding place?

Should not the heart be bitter
To feel the time at hand
When he will try my slipper
On all throughout the land?

1913

*

I've a certain smile — you can see
Almost no lip movement at all.
I preserve it for you — after all,
It was love that gave it to me.
Never mind you are wicked and crude,
Never mind you love others besides,
Gold before me are altar and rood,
Close beside me the groom of grey eyes.

1913

So I took my love out to the entry,
And I lingered where the sun-motes gleamed.
Floating from the nearby belfry,
Consequential tollings streamed.
Left! Incongruous expression, really—
What am I, a letter, a bouquet?
And my eyes already gaze severely
In the mirror's gathering gray.

1913

*

By smells of blooming things and dead
This home is pleasantly pervaded.
All bright against each black-earth bed
Heaped vegetables have been spaded.

The air still runs with veins of cool,
But hot-beds glint, no longer padded.
There is a pool, the kind of pool
Whose muddy slicknesses look plaided.

A boy had seen beneath its glass
And whispers to me in a sweat
That in there lives a giant bass
With his enormous bassinette.

1913

*

In servitude you know I languish,
For leave to die I plead with God,
But always, to the edge of anguish,
I see the Tver-land's grudging sod.

A weathered well with hauling-crane,
Above it clouds, like vapor leaking,
Out in the fields the stile-gates creaking,
And heartache—in the fragrant grain.

Those unspectacular expanses
Where even winds dare not alarm,
And those evaluating glances
Of countrywomen tanned and calm.

Autumn, 1913

*

The pale flag, on the customshouse blowing;
Over town hangs a yellowish stain.
More on guard now, my heart is slowing
Its beat, and to sigh is pain.

Be again a young seaside slattern,
Slip sandals over bare toes,
Braid my hair in a coronet pattern,
And sing out as my throbbing voice chose!

From the porch, see dun cupolas arching
Up the Khersones temple-roof's slope,
Unaware that renown and good fortune
Wither hearts so beyond any hope.

1913

*

Ski tracks will be drily crackling—
Oh, I know, I know.
Amber moon on dark-blue backing,
At a lovely tilt the snow.

All the palace lights are twinkling,
Silence set them farther back.
Pathless, trackless, not an inkling,
Just some iceholes yawning black.

Stand not in my way, o willow,
Where the lake-maids nest!
On your snowy twigs for pillow
Dawbirds, small black dawbirds rest.

Tsarskoe Selo
October, 1913

*

True tenderness there's no aping,
It tells, though it hardly stirs.
No use your carefully draping
My shoulders and breast in furs.
And no use your abjectly serving
First-love talk which reassures.
How well I know these unswerving,
These ravenous looks of yours!

December, 1913

from WHITE FLOCK

Weak is my voice, but my resolve is steady,
Now love is gone, I even feel relieved.
Deep is the sky, the wind blows high and heady,
In purity are all my thoughts conceived.

My night-nurse, sleeplessness, has left my bower,
Nor do I mourn gray ashes as before,
The crooked clock-hand poised upon the tower
Is not a deadly arrow any more.

How that long grip upon the heart is ending!
Release is near. I pardon everything,
Just following a ray of sun, ascending
And running down the ivy-slide of spring.

Tsarskoe Selo, 1912

*

You don't come to my mind very often,
I don't pore over all that you do,
But an imprint is there and won't soften
Of that trivial meeting with you.

Your red house on the turbid river,
Your red house I consistently shun,
Yet I know I set sorely aquiver
Your repose saturated with sun.

Not that ever your lips, love-haunted,
Did over my lips incline,
Ardent verses of yours ever granted
Life eternal to yearnings of mine—

Yet my spells probe the future in secret,
When the evening is utterly blue,
I feel sure of a second meeting,
Ineluctable meeting with you.

1913

Seclusion

There is no single stone at which I cower,
So many have by now been cast at me,
From spent assault has grown a handsome tower,
Aloft among the lofty ones you see.
I render thanks to those who built it so,
May they be spared anxiety and grieving.
Up here the morning sun is first to glow,
Here shine the sunset glories last in leaving.
And in my room, the windows oftentimes
Breathe in the ocean winds of northern climes,
A dove will peck from thumb and fingers wheat...
And any page that I left incomplete—
Divinely imperturbable and light,
The Muse's tawny hand will set it right.

Slepnevo
Summer, 1914

*

You are hard, love recalled! On your pyre
I am cast to be song and live coal,
While to others—there's merely a fire
To lend warmth to the burned-out soul.

For their surfeited bodies to waken,
By my tears they need to be stung...
For this, God, have I partaken
Of love, then? For this have I sung?

Make me swallow of such a poison
As will leave me bereft of speech,
And my infamous fame's loud noising
In illumined oblivion leach.

1914

First my halcyon cradle were you,
Sombre town on the menacing current,
And my jubilant wedding-couch too,
Where the young seraphim of your warrant
Held the marriage crown steady above,
City loved with a rancorous love.

And my suppliant orisons' kneeler
Were you, quiet, beclouded, austere.
And here first did my chosen, revealer
Of my shimmering path, appear,
And behind the sad Muse I glided
At her hand, as the blind are guided.

1914

*

Kiev

My arrival here is haunting,
Kiev seems forlorn—
By his stream Vladimir flaunting
His black cross upborne,

Elm and linden murmurs drifting
From the darkened parks,
Stars to the Almighty lifting
Bristling diamond sparks.

Grief and glory's shifting sequel,
I will end it there,
With me none but you, my equal,
And the love I bear.

1914

Parting

Twilit and downward turning
I see my path ahead.
Just yesterday, still burning,
"Do not forget" he said.
Now all I had is leveled
But winds, and shepherd's cries,
And cedar trees disheveled
Where limpid waters rise.

1914

*

The lanterns burn yellow and fresh. The walk
Through the seaside garden is dim.
I'm very calm. I'd just rather not talk
With anyone about him.

You're dear and steady, we shall be friends...
Go strolling, kiss, grow older...
And months will flutter end to end
Like snow-stars over our shoulder.

1914

*

A frosty sun. Treading, treading,
Soldiers return from parade.
The January noon feels heady,
I'm almost unafraid.

I recall every branch in this setting,
Every silhouette I know.

Through the hoarfrost's snow-white netting
Filters a crimson glow.

Here the house stood, white, or nearly,
And the glass porch. Who could tell
How often my hand, all chilly,
Has clung to the grip of that bell.

How often.... Buglers, go jangling,
I'm off to seek out my place,
I will tell by the gables' angling,
By the evergreen up its face.

But oh, it must have been shifted
To strange towns by a force of some kind,
Or the way how to go there lifted
Forever out of my mind.

Pipes fade far off; with a motion
Like cherry-bloom, snowflakes veer...
Not a soul, you can tell, has a notion
The white house is gone from here.

1914

*

Consolation

> *There Arch-Commander Michael*
> *Enrolled him in his Host.*
>   N. Gumilev

He will not be sending you any more letters,
There will be no word or sound.
In Poland, ablaze at the stake in fetters,
You will scarcely find his mound.

Now be you still and calm in spirit,
There's no more loss to be borne:
He's a warrior in God's battalion of merit,
Not now for you to mourn.

In his own dear house it's sinful to sorrow,
Sinful for heart to faint.
Just think, you may pray for succor tomorrow
To your own dear patron saint.

1914

*

To My Love

Do not send a pigeon down my way,
Do not write me worried letters please,
Waft not in my face the wind of March.
For I entered Heaven yesterday,
Where both soul and body came to ease
Underneath a shady poplar arch.

I can see our town, the palace towers,
Barrack wings, and sentry booths from here,
And the yellow Ming bridge spanning ice.
You've awaited me for freezing hours;
Loath to leave my porch, you linger near,
Marveling how the stars grew thick as rice.

I will climb an alder, squirrel-gray,
As a wary weasel scamper through,
As a swan will call you to my side,
Lest my plighted lover know dismay,
Shivering in a swirl of snowy blue,
Waiting for his plighted love who died.

Tsarskoe Selo
February, 1915

I don't know, are you dead, are you living,—
Is it proper to search for you here,
Or through posthumous twilights given
To musing as bright as a tear.

All is yours: daily praying for mercies,
My insomnia's feverish haze,
And the white-winged swarm of my verses,
And the flare of my deep-blue gaze.

There is none I have held more precious,
There is none has so harrowed my lot,
Not who cast me in torture's meshes,
Not who fondled me and forgot.

1915

*

The evening light is ripe and clear,
The touch of April's cool caressing.
You are late to come by many a year,
But still to me you come a blessing.

Come here, sit close to me and look,
Just send a twinkle upon some pages:
Look at this dark-blue copybook,
My girlhood verse in all its stages.

Forgive my having done much grieving
And found small joy in skies of blue.
Forgive, forgive me for believing
Too many others to be you.

1915

N. V. N.

All growing closer ends upon a fateful verge,
Not to be cheated by inloveness and possession—
However lip and lip in awesome silence merge,
And heart would burst in two from love's oppression.

Without avail are either friendship here
Or years when happiness is high and fervent,
Years when the spirit is unbound and clear,
To lust's slow-dragging languor not a servant.

Whoever strives for it is mindless, and he who
Attains to it is by despair unmanned...
Now you have understood why it is true
My heart declines to beat beneath your hand.

May, 1915
Petersburg

*

He never did praise or chide me,
As will foes or friends, you see,
He just left his soul beside me
And said: you keep it for me.

And now it has been my worry,
What if his time runs out?
One of God's archangels will hurry
My way for his soul, no doubt.

How then would I hide it, vainly,
Keep it dark from the cherubim?
When its song and its sob so plainly
Proclaim it of Heaven and Him.

1915

Like a bride I get each day
A letter handed here,
Late at night I have my say
Answering my dear.

"Death in white is who I stay with
On my way to dark.
Any ill on earth repay with
Good, beloved, mark!"

And a star is standing, lofty,
In between two boles,
Pledging dream-fulfillment softly
To all slumbering souls.

October, 1915
Hüvinkka

*

Yet somewhere life is simple, after all,
A light to warm and cheer and glisten...
A neighbor there at dusk across the wall
Chats with a girl, with only bees to listen
To this, the tenderest talk of all.

The life we lead is decorous and wearing,
Our bitter trysts impend, like rites to preach,
While with its gusts a harebrained wind is tearing
The clauses off a scarcely started speech.

For nothing, though, are we prepared to lose
Our granite city great with fame and woes,
Its spreading rivers with their crystal floes,
The gloomy gardens' dusky green repose,
And those but half-heard accents of the Muse.

1915

Beneath the chill roof of my empty lair
I count not the days that are hollow,
The Apostles' Letters I study there,
The words of the Psalmodist follow.
But blue are the stars, the frost all lace,
New marvels each tryst heaps on,—
In the Book a red maple leaf marks the place
Of the High Song of Solomon.

1915

*

When I shall be resting calmly
Six feet down in oaken shell,
You'll come skipping to your Mummy
Of a Sunday for a spell.
Cross the brook and up the hillside,
Leaving grown-ups at a loss,
From afar, my precious, lynx-eyed,
You will recognize my cross.
Things remembered that evoke me
Will be precious few, I'd say:
Did not scold me, did not stroke me,
Let me off Communion day.

1915

*

The immortelles are dry and pink. The clouds
Upon the laundered sky are roughly molded,
The leaves still blossomless and half unfolded
Upon the single oak-tree hereabouts.

Midnight, and sunset rays still here to see.
How snug it is, my tightly jointed carvel!

About all kind of loveliness and marvel
The birds of the Almighty speak to me.

I'm happy here. But dearest to my heart
I hold the sloping forest trail, the brittle
Untidy bridge that seems to sag a little,
And that from which I'm only days apart.

1916

*

I know that you are my reward
For years of suffering and dearth,
For never having grubbed a hoard
Of the amenities of earth,
For my unwillingness to call
"I care" to one I love and miss,
For my forgiving all to all,
You'll be the angel of my bliss.

1916

*

To M. Lozinsky

They're only on their way here, swiftly winging,
The words of love and of deliverance,
And I've worked up my turmoil-before-singing
Already, and my icy lips are tense.

But presently—where meager birches dangle,
With bony rustle leaning on the pane,
To wreaths of golden-red will roses tangle,
And speech of the unseen be rendered plain.

And then—the world is prodigal past bearing,
Intoxicates like ruby-red hot wine...
The herald wind, its glow and fragrance sharing,
Has with its sough already seared my mind.

Slepnevo
Summer, 1916

*

All promised him to me: the rim
Of heaven, dusky-red and golden,
At Christmas time a sunny dream,
The wind of Easter, bell-beholden.

The waterfalls of garden size,
The purple saplings of the thicket,
The pair of mighty dragonflies
Perched on a rusty iron wicket.

I never merely nourished hope
That he would come and be my own,
As I would walk the mountain slope
Along the flaming path of stone.

1916

*

Like a white stone far down a well-shaft sighted,
Deep in myself a memory has lain.
I cannot and I do not want to fight it:
It is a thing of joy, and it is pain.

I feel that anyone who might be glancing
Into my eyes must see it without fail,

And turn more sadly pensive than one chancing
To listen to some agonizing tale.

I know that the Olympians used to alter
Men into things, yet leave them conscious, too.
To make these wondrous sorrows never falter,
You're turned into my memory of you.

Slepnevo
Summer, 1916

*

In Memoriam, July 19, 1914

We grew a hundred years in age, and all
Within a single hour, it seemed:
Brief summer merged already into fall,
The open flanks of ploughed-up acres steamed.

And of a sudden bloomed the quiet road,
A sobbing went, as with a silvery crack.
I covered up my face, imploring God
To strike me dead before the first attack.

Swept off, as trappings out of place and flighty,
Were shades of song and passion—and instead
The mind was reordained by the Almighty
For thunderous tidings as an archive dread.

1916

*

All has been stripped away: both love and strength.
The body, tossed into this town unwilling,
Sulks at the sunshine, and I sense at length
The blood run cold in me, to utmost chilling.

Where is my Muse's gaiety and zest?
She gazes, but her lips remain unstirred,
Her garland-shaded head, without a word,
Droops, sadly overcome, against my breast.

I only feel more fiercely conscience-ridden
With each new day: it wants a mighty prize.
I make some answer, with my face well hidden,
But here's an end to tears and alibis.

Sevastopol
24 October, 1916

*

Statue In Tsarskoe Selo

To N. V. Nedobrovo

Already gleams the lake of swans
With falling maple foliage wrinkled,
The slowly-ripening rowan's fronds
About the banks are blood-besprinkled.

And dazzling on her northern stone,
Legs crossed which rigors never harden,
She peers in slimness all her own
Upon the pathways of the garden.

I was obscurely seized with fright
Before this legendary maiden.
About her shoulders played the light
Of grudging autumn, slowly fading.

And how forgive her, having borne
The fervor of your praise enamored...
For her, you see, it's fun to mourn
In nakedness so all-englamored.

Autumn, 1916

Song About a Song

Its iciness will seem to sear
Like frozen wind, to start,
Then as a single salty tear
Drop down into the heart.

And the wicked heart will bear regret
Somehow, and smart tomorrow,
And vainly struggle to forget
The subtly nagging sorrow.

I only sow. The reaping's done
By later comers. And?
I ask your blessing, Lord, upon
The reapers' larking band.

So that I dare to render, then,
More perfect thanks above,
Allow me to bestow on men
That which outlasts all love.

1916

*

As I arrive there my vexations flee me,
I gladly welcome early winter chills,
The swarthy hamlets, secretive and dreamy,
Are toil and prayer's sheltering domicils.

Love for these parts, held calmly and securely,
Will always ineluctably be mine:
A drop of blood of Novgorod is surely
Afloat in me like ice in foaming wine.

This crystal will not thaw to any searing,
The hottest ever has not seen it done,
Whatever else I may have started cheering—
You shimmer forth before me, quiet one.

1916

*

For Yunia Anrep

Is it my circumstances that have changed,
Or fun and games are really gone?
Where are those winters when my bedtime ranged
From six a.m. to dawn?

To calmer, sterner living I surrender,
Set down upon an uncouth shore,
And speeches lackadaisical or tender
Will pass across my lips no more.

One can't believe that Christmas is in reach.
The steppe looks touching, green with turf.
The sun is brilliant. Up the glassy beach
There seems to surge a warming surf.

At times when I was overcome and languid
With bliss, it was of such a quiet shoal
I used to dream with tremulous abandon,
And just like this it was I then imagined
The wandering of the newly risen soul.

Sevastopol
December, 1916

Blessing of the Lord, the morning's beam
Glided down my lover's face; the sleeper
Looked a little paler in his dream,
But his slumber presently grew deeper.

Warmly wandering, that ray of heaven
Must have felt to him like lover's nips;
Just so with my mouth I used to travel
Down his tawny shoulders and dear lips.

Now, more disembodied than a spirit,
In my grief no wandering can allay,
Only as a song I fly to visit,
And caress him as a morning ray.

1916

*

O there are words which do not flow anew,
Who speaks them—spends what he can ill afford.
For inexhaustible is but the blue
Of heaven and the mercy of the Lord.

Sevastopol
Winter, 1916

*

Here, you would say, the voice of mortals
Will never echo, here alone
There grimly rams at sable portals
The gale-wind of an age of stone.
And I alone seem left to suffer
Survival in this stark design—
For having been the first to offer
To take a draught of deadly wine.

1917

We haven't the knack of parting,
And, shoulder to shoulder, just walk.
New day is already starting;
You're preoccupied; I don't talk.

We enter a church, where the fathers
Wed, christen, send Dust to Dust;
As we leave we don't look at each other...
Why is everything wrong for us?

Or we sit on a churchyard's thawing
Snow-sheets, sigh lightly and gaze
At the mansions your cane-tip is drawing
Where it shall be we two, always.

1917

*

My shadow has remained behind there, staying
Still in the same blue room with its chagrin,
It waits a midnight guest from town and, praying,
Its lips touch on a saint of lacquered tin.
Nor is the house now altogether cheery:
They light the fire and yet the place stays dim...
Is this why the new lady's eyes look weary,
And why the master keeps the wine by him
And hears the one who's paying me that call
Converse with me behind the flimsy wall?

1917

It is nighttime. The twenty-first. Monday.
The lines of the city fog-furled.
Some young ne'erdowell improvised one day
That there's something called love in the world.

And from slackness or out of frustration,
All believed it and now follow suit:
Make assignments and dread separation
And go caroling love-songs to boot.

But the truth of the matter will surface
For some in a speechless spell....
I chanced on it, quite without purpose,
And ever since haven't been well.

1917

*

A. L.

I liked our gatherings in the nightly world—
Small table, frosted glasses and decanter,
Black cups with fragrant vapor overcurled,
The chimney with its massive winter blast,
The stinging zest of literary banter
And love's first look, both fearsome and aghast.

1917

Spring, the mysterious, still languished newly,
Transparent mountain breezes roved the land,
And on its depth the lake face glistened bluely,
The Christener's shrine not made by human hand.

I prayed already for the second meeting
While you were still in terror at the one,
And here, today, another torrid evening—
How low upon the hill now hangs the sun...

You are not with me, yet there was no parting,
To me each moment is in triumph writ.
I know there is in you such anguished smarting
That not a word can pass your lips for it.

Spring, 1917

*

from WAYSIDE HERB

How grimly is my body stunted,
The pain-racked lips a withered slit!
Not this has been the death I wanted,
Not this the time I chose for it.
I thought, of cloud and cloud colliding
A clash on high would come to be,
And lightening blazes swiftly riding,
And voice of mighty joy abiding,
Like angels, would descend on me.

1913

*

A string of beads about the throat,
A wide muff for my hands to creep in,
An absentminded gaze afloat
In eyes no longer used for weeping.

My face seems of paler tinge
Than silk of lilac opalescence,
Down nearly to the brows my fringe
Has lowered its untended crescents.

My step is halting, too, and slow,
Bears scant affinity to soaring,
As though I walked a raft below
And not these squares of parquet flooring;

Pale lips wrung half apart with ache,
Laborious breath, inert and fleeting,
And limply at my bosom shake
The flowers of that abortive meeting.

1913

Earth's fame is a smoky pall,
Not this did I importune.
Unto my lovers all
I brought the best of fortune.
One is alive and in bonds
Of romance to his lady fair,
The other has turned to bronze
In a snowed-up public square.

1914

*

My dreams could frequent you more rarely,
As much as we meet in the day;
But only in night's dim aerie
Are you wistful, or tender, or gay.
More sweetly than angel-song befuddle.
Your lips with their flattery dear... --
No getting my first name muddled,
Or heaving the sighs you do here.

1914

*

Like an angel, quiet waters scoring,
You bent down into my face to see,
And, my strength and liberty restoring,
Took a ring to mark the prodigy.
My hot flushes, feverish and morbid—
God-beseeching woe has scoured them off.
In my mind this month will live, the turbid
Arctic February, blizzard-rough.

Tsarskoe Selo
February, 1916

Here am I, left alone to string
Blank days like bead to bead.
O friends, at large, free-wandering,
My wayward swans, o heed!

To call you down my song lacks power,
My tears won't turn your aim,
But of a mournful evening hour
My prayer will speak your name.

One, struck by deadly arrow-tip,
Fell plummeting aback,
Another, having kissed my lip,
Became a raven black.

But once a year it happens, mark—
The time the ice-sheet thaws,
That in imperial Catherine's park
By waters bright I pause,

And hear broad pinions plash and lift
Above the azure swell.
I wonder who has struck a rift
In the sepulchral cell.

1916

*

I left my window naked,
My room lies bare to all eyes.
That now you can't forsake it
To me is a gay surprise.
Go, mutter of hoydens and heedlessness,
Go on, make a furious scene:
I'll still have been your sleeplessness,
Your discontent have I been.

1916

On the crest of a hard-frozen snow ridge,
To my white and mysterious home,
So hushed, you and I, by our knowledge,
In intimate silence we come.
To me this fulfillment is sweeter
Than all I have thought of to sing—
And the branches we brush, and their teeter,
And your spurs with their delicate ring.

January, 1917

*

The time he ultimately comes to learn
Of my remote and miserable ending,
Not soberer or sadder will he turn,
But smile a little, pale and condescending.
Right then, grey skies will come to him, all cloud,
And snow-whirls down Neva's embankment snarling,
Right then he will remember how he vowed
To cherish and protect his eastern darling.

1917

*

I hear the oriole, its fluting ever plangent,
And summer's pageantry I hasten to dismiss,
As wheat-ears, each to others tightly tangent,
The sickle severs with a serpent hiss.

Slim reapers, skimpy skirt-tails at an angle,
Flap in the wind like flags on holidays,
This calls for merry harness-bells to jangle,
While dusty lashes shade a lingering gaze.

I seek for no caress, no lovers' meeting,
Aware of doom not to be banished hence
But come and let us look again at Eden,
Where we were one in bliss and innocence.

Summer, 1917

*

The river dawdles, valley waters gathering;
Half up the slope, a many-windowed hall.
We might be living in the reign of Catherine,
Holding devotions and awaiting fall.
A gulf of two days' absence bridged, a caller
Comes cantering up through where the barley burns:
He kisses Grandma's hand in the front parlor,
And then my lips, up where the staircase turns.

Summer, 1917

*

No one will listen now to songs. The tragic,
So long foreshadowed days have come around.
You, my last song, the world has lost its magic,
Please do not tear my heart in two—don't sound.

Not long ago, a carefree little swallow
Who on her early outing skims and soars,
And now, a beggar maiden wan and sallow,
Who taps in vain on other people's doors.

1917

You stay new, your secrets grow not lesser,
My surrenders daily more entire.
But that love of yours, o dear oppressor,
Is ordeal by iron and by fire.

Smiling and the sound of songs you veto,
Prayer has long before been barred.
Just let nothing part us is my credo,
All the rest will not be hard.

Stranger to the realms of earth and heaven
I am living now and sing no more,
Just as if my free soul had been riven
From both Hell and Heaven on your score.

December, 1917

*

With a ringing the ice-floes pour,
The high heavens are hopelessly pale.
Won't you tell what you punish me for?
I don't know where it is I fail.

Kill me, do, if it has to be,
But do not be harsh with me first.
You don't want any children from me
And you do not like my verse.

I am true to my pledged belief,
By your say-so let everything be!
I did give you my life, but grief
I will take to the grave with me.

April, 1918

From your love with its constant riddle
I cry out aloud as if stung,
I have turned all sallow and brittle,
Barely dragging my feet along.

Don't twitter me up new songbooks,
For how long do they cheat, at best?
But more fiercely claw with your strong hooks,
Claw up my consumptive chest,

To send blood from the torn throat gushing
The faster on sheet and rug,
To make death at the last come flushing
My heart of its odious drug.

July, 1918

*

from ANNO DOMINI

That August, like yellow flame searing
Its way through a smoky haze,
That August rose over us rearing,
A seraph of fiery blaze.

The city of wrath and sorrow,
From quiet Carelia borne,
We entered, maiden and warrior,
At the break of a frigid dawn.

What struck our great city, what stranded
The sun from its blinding height?
The eagle in black on the standard
Now strained like a bird in flight.

Now barbarous bivouacs littered
Those vistas that ravished the eye,
Spiked helmets and bayonets glittered,
Bedazzling the passer-by.

From Troitsky Bridge dull thunder
Of cannon wheels rolled and churned,
In the Summer Park, furled in wonder,
The linden had not yet turned.

And then my brother told me:
These are great days for me.
Now you preserve and hold me
Our griefs, our ecstasy.

As if to the chatelaine leaving
The keys to his home domain,
While eastern winds were sleaving
The reeds of the Volga plain.

1915

Weathered rusty and gnarled is the log-timbered span,
And the burdock is grown to the height of a man,
Supple forests of sibilant nettles veer,
Much too rank for the scythe to go in and shear.
At the twilight the lake sends a sigh across,
And the sides of the bridge are tousled with moss.

    Here my twenty-first
    Birthday did I meet.
    Heady honey-taste
    To my lips was sweet.

    From my silken sheath
    Briars ripped the frill,
    Songbirds in the leaf
    Never ceased to trill.

    At my hail he stole
    From the lair beyond,
    Uncouth as a troll,
    Than a child more fond.

    Racing up the slant,
    Swimming through the loch,
    Just for that I shan't
    Later say: enough.

1917

*

Phantom

The pendant hemispheres of light
From lanterns early lit are jangling,
More festive ever and more bright,
The snowflakes glitter, past them angling.

And, speeding up their even flow
As if they sensed pursuers chasing,
Across the softly falling snow,
Beneath blue netting, steeds are racing.

A haiduk, gold-gallooned, stands out
Erect behind the sleigh, unshaken,
And strangely peers the Tsar about
From irises alight and vacant.

1919

*

For N. V. Rykova-Gukovskaya

All is looted, betrayed, past retrieving,
Death's black wing has been flickering near,
All is racked with a ravenous grieving,
How on earth did this splendor appear?

In the daylight a fragrance of cherry
Wafts from fabulous woods nearby,
In the darkness new star-guilds ferry
The luminous night of July.

Oh, the wondrous draws closer ever
To the hovels of rubble and grime,
Known to no one and witnessed never,
But sought out from the onset of time.

1921

If life were just tomorrow-free!
In every word I savor treason,
This is the star-rise of a season
That augurs waning love to me.

Take off unseen; if thrown together,
Not recognize him, almost miss.
But then—comes night. Those shoulders ever
In liquid lassitude to kiss.

You did not hold me dear at all,
I cooled to you. The torture dragged,
And like a convict, love has fagged
His labor on, perfused with gall.

A brother now; you're silent, frown.
And yet, if but our eyes should meet,
I swear by Heaven's Judgment Seat
The blaze would melt a boulder down.

1921

*

Hark, kind wanderer, though distant,
What I plead with you about,
In the sky new candles glisten,
Sky that sees the sunset out.

Quick, dear wanderer, I am guiding
Your bright gazes hither—see
Here a crafty dragon biding
Who has long been lord of me.

And within the dragon's cavern
Neither law nor mercy govern,
And a lash hangs on a ring
For the songs I must not sing.

Wingéd dragon racks the body,
Humbleness he has me study,
So, my brazen laugh suppressed,
I'll be better than the rest.

Wanderer mine, to our far city
Carry these my words and give
What should stab the one with pity
But for whom I would not live.

June, 1921

*

So you thought me the standard romantic,
To be dropped and forgotten, of course;
That I'd fling myself, sobbing and frantic,
To the hooves of a runaway horse.

Or I'd go to a wise-woman peasant
For persuading decoctions of wort,
And would send you a frightening present,
Like my kerchief all perfumed with hurt.

Be accursed, then. Nor moaning nor gazes
To the reprobate soul will I turn,
But I swear by the shrine's sacred hazes,
By the grove where the angels sojourn,
By the fume of our sensuous blazes—
I have gone and shall never return.

July, 1921

*

So we somehow contrived to be severed,
And to snuff the dim spark in the glove.
It were time for you, hated forever,
To be learning how truly to love.

I am free now. And, keeping my fun up,
In the night-time the Muse wings me cheer,
And ambition lopes round with the sun-up
And goes rattling its beads in my ear.

It's not worth it to pray for me even,
Or look back as you go on your way.
The black wind will assuage me on leaving,
And the gold of the fall make my day.

I'll count riddance a gift of good fortune,
And oblivion a generous boon.
Tell me, though, dare you visit that torture
Of the damned on another girl soon?

August, 1921

*

So once again send organ voices crashing,
As thunderclouds in early spring collide—
My level-lidded gazes will be flashing
Behind the shoulder of your chosen bride.

Seven days of love, seven years apart—and shattered
By hideous war, upheaval, home a shard,
With guiltless blood the slender fingers spattered,
With silver strand the rosy temple marred.

Good-bye, farewell, be glad, my dear, my handsome,
I yield the cherished pledge you gave me then;
But dare not pass to your flushed bride for ransom
My frenzy, not to be essayed again—

For it would penetrate with venom ardent
Your prosperous, your blithely savored thrall...
While I would go and tend my magic garden,
Where grasses whisper, and the Muses call.

1921

A cast-iron enclosure,
A cot of yellow pine.
What bliss that jealous torture
No longer shall be mine.

They straighten now this bedding
For me with sobs and prayer;
God speed—now make your heading
Wherever wind is fair!

Now frenzy ceases rending
Your ear with gales of spite,
Now no one will be tending
A candle through the night.

We've found a vestal spirit,
And calmness that endures...
You cry—I do not merit
A single tear of yours.

1921

*

Until, sunken down in some clearing,
I perish of wind and of rain,
The dream of deliverance nearing
Burns on like some curse in my brain.

I wait, and with stubborn endurance
Enlist what is song in my cause,
He'll knock at the door, all assurance,
And morning-like, gay, as he was,

He enters, he says "It's all buried,
See, I have forgiven it too."
All done being frightened and harried...
No roses, no bolts from the blue.

If, crazed with dark anguish, within it
I still save my heart, this is why:
Deprived of the bliss of that minute
I just cannot see myself die.

August, 1921

*

From the shining threshold of Heaven
He called back: "I'll be waiting here!"
As he died he enjoined my living
In dearth with bounty and cheer.

Now, a highwind his pinions flaring,
He looks down a diaphanous sky
At the crust of bread I am sharing
With those more needy than I.

And when, as after hard fighting,
Clouds welter in blood above,
He feels my prayers alighting
And hears the words of my love.

1921

*

I augured my loved ones undoing,
And in swathes they perished away.
Ah wretched me! All this ruin
Obeyed my prefiguring sway.
As odor of hot fresh carrion
The ravens will circle above,
So sent its verses harrying,
Exultantly, my fierce love.

You're close to me, glowing and balmy,
I feel you heart-deep in my breast.
Give your hand, listen carefully, calmly.
I beg you: go off, it is best.
Keep dark from me where you are going.
Don't call on him, Muse, not a sign.
Let him live unsung and unknowing,
Unrent by that love of mine.

1921

*

The cathedral doors are flung wide open,
Linden trees stand beggared to the bark,
And the gilt along the inward-sloping
Immemorial masonry is dark.

Droning smothers vaulted arch and chapel,
Past the Dniepr wing off the mighty sounds.
Thus the massive king-bell of Mazepa
High atop St. Sophie's square resounds.

Ever more implacably it bellows,
As if heretics were harrowed here,
By the far bank's forest, though, it mellows
And bestows on fluffy fox-cubs cheer.

1921

*

Tear-sodden autumn, like a widow sheathed
In weeds of black, all happy vision blearing,
And idly shuffling over words bequeathed,
Forever sobbing, never clearing...

Nor will it change until most stealthy snow
Takes pity on the wan, forsaken wife...
Release from ecstasy, release from woe—
No little thing to barter for your life.

1921.

*

Me, honor and obey? You've lost your mind!
I only heed what the Almighty utters.
I have no use for suffering or flutters,
Husband spells headsman to me, housed—confined.

But now, you see? All on my own I came;
It grew December, piercing winds had risen,
It was so brightly cheerful in your prison,
And darkness yawned behind the window frame.

Like this, against a bright transparent pane
A bird will thrust itself as blizzards riot,
Its white wing darkening with a bloody stain.

Now I am filled with happiness and quiet.
Ciaou, restful one—I'll hold you ever dear
For having let a pilgrim shelter here.

1921

*

Far-Off Voice, I

He said for him I was the peerless one,
My essence meant, unlike an earthly woman's,
The shimmering solace of the winter sun,
His native music with its savage summons.

He said that if I died he would not grieve
Or cry "rise up again", by demons driven,
But would know instantly one cannot live
Flesh without sun, or soul from music riven.
...And now?

1921

*

I have seen it, that gold-hammered wreath,
And I say, do not hanker for it.
It's the ill-gotten goods of a thief,
And besides would not suit you a bit.
As a hard-twisted briar-thorn bough
Shall my wreath come to glitter on you;
What's the odds if your delicate brow
Is encrimsoned with freshening dew.

1921 (?)

*

With earthly comforts do not freight your heart,
Let wife nor house engross you to a passion,
Take up the bread that is your own child's part
And hand it over for a stranger's ration.
This season serve as meekest underling
Him who was dust beneath you at another,
And call the wild beast of the forest brother,
And do not ask the Lord for anything.

1922

I am no kin to those who left you,
My land, to preying foemen's wrongs.
Their coarse enticements I am deaf to,
Nor will I give them of my songs.

The outcast, though, I sorrow over
As one shut in, confined to bed.
For darkness shades your path, poor rover,
Of wormwood tastes the exile's bread.

Yet here...the last of youth conceded
To Armageddon's smouldering glow,
We for our part have not succeeded
In warding off a single blow.

By later minds—one may be fearless—
Each hour will be accounted just...
Meanwhile, the world holds none more tearless,
More arrogant, more plain than us.

1922

*

O stop pacing, all unpivoted,
One foot here and one in flight!
Yes—a single soul is riveted
On us two—you got it right.

I'll be good to you, yes, I'll cosset you,
It's the most undreamt-of thing;
Try to lash me if I fuss at you—
You yourself will feel the sting.

1922

Breezes as of swanny rivers;
In the blood, the blue above.
Anniversaries are with us
Of the first-days of your love.

All my sorcery you prisoned,
And the years like water ran.
How is it you are not wizened,
But the same as you were then?

Gentle voice more fully rounded,
Only time's grey wind has now
With a lovely snowburst bounded
The serenely tranquil brow.

1922

*

The angel who guarded me for three years
Soared up in a glory of rays;
I patiently wait for the sweetest of days,
The day that he reappears.

What hollow cheeks, what a bloodless lip,
My face nobody would know;
I'm lovely no more, after all, not the slip
Whose song could startle him so.

I've long had nothing on earth to fear,
Recalling his words at the door.
I'll bow to his feet as he enters here,
Where I barely nodded before.

1922 (?)

To fall sick now, delirium, what fun—
To be meeting them all again,
In the park by the sea, full of wind and sun,
Taking this and the other broad lane.

Then the very departed consent to throng,
And the exiles, my no-man's land.
Won't you lead up the little one by the hand,
I have missed him so much, so long?

I will eat blue grapes from my lover's hands,
I will drink with him icy wine,
And look on as the hoar-maned waterfall's strands
Into brimming shingle-beds twine.

1922 (?)

*

Beyond the lake the waning moon has slowed,
And stands there like a window open wide
Into a hushed and brightly lit abode
Where something dreadful has occurred inside.

The master has been carried home for dead,
The mistress has absconded with a lover,
Or a small girl is lost, and they discover
A little slipper by the river-bed...

From earth you cannot tell. But some appalling
Misfortune sensing, we had fallen quiet.
Placatingly the eagle owls were calling,
And in the park a sultry wind ran riot.

1922

For V. K. Shileyko

Had you forgotten, free and firm one,
To those caressing knees a prey,
That the primeval sin will earn one
Annihilation and decay?

Why give her for a bedside story
The code to wonder-working days—
Her, who will dissipate your glory
With her expropriating ways?

For shame—the fruitful sadness never
Through earthly woman seek to wake.
Such have been shut in cloisters ever
Or burnt to cinders at the stake.

1922

*

Lot's Wife

> *But his wife looked back from behind*
> *him, and she became a pillar of salt.*
> Genesis

The just man strode after God's messenger proudly,
Prodigious and bright, along mountains of black.
But aching unease to his lady spoke loudly:
There's time yet—it wasn't too late to look back

On the stately red towers of the Sodom she fled now,
The court of her singing, the hall where she span,
The goodly high mansion, its window-gaps dead now,
Wherein she gave birth for the love of a man.

She looked—and by lethal oblivion assaulted,
Her eyes lost the art to take in any more;

To luminous rock-salt her body was altered,
Her nimble feet merged with the quartz of the tor.

Who weeps for the woman, who thinks to regret her?
Who does not account her the less for her lack?
My own heart alone cannot ever forget her,
Who laid down her life for a single glance back.

1922-24

*

Here's the shore, then, of the northern ocean,
Here's the bar our griefs and glories meet—
Is it bliss or sorrow, that emotion
That has flung you weeping to my feet?

I don't fancy any more condemned men,
Convicts, hostages, or slaves—instead
Only with my lover, one unbending,
Will I share both roof and daily bread.

1922

*

It is fine here: all rustle and creak,
With each morning the frost only grows,
Flaming white hangs a bush, frozen sleek,
In a dazzle of rose upon rose.
Down this holiday glory of snow
Runs a ski-track, as if it would try
To recall that dim ages ago
We went walking this way, you and I.

1922

from BULRUSHES

The Muse

When nights I wait for her epiphany,
Life seems suspended by a hair, and moot.
What's honors, being young, and feeling free,
Before this dear guest with her shepherd's flute.

And here she was. She gazed at me and waited
Attentively, her veil tossed overhead.
I ask her: "Was it you then who dictated
The script of Hell to Dante?" "I," she said.

1924

*

This is where Pushkin's exile was begun,
This is where that of Lermontov was ended.
The highland herbs up here are lightly scented,
And it was but a single time I won
A glimpse into the shore's deep plane-tree cover,
And on that westering and ruthless hour
Saw the indomitable glinting glower,
The eye-light of Tamara's deathless lover.

Kislovodsk, 1927

*

When the bane of the moon is at work,
Town is steeped in its venomous potion.
No illusions of sleep still lurk,
And I see through the lurid murk
Not my childhood, and not the ocean,
Not the butterflies' wedding swarm, once
Over snowy-white daffodils vaulted,

Was it nineteen-sixteen, perchance,—
But the cypresses' choral dance
On your grave-mound, forever halted.

1928

*

That town of mine, from childhood cherished,
In its December hush of gray
Seemed to reveal itself my perished,
Misspent inheritance today.

All that was showered on heart unheeding,
And was so lightly passed along:
The spirit's fervor, notes of pleading,
The blessedness of maiden song—

A wispy effluence, had dwindled
In mirror depths, dissolved to haze...
Of that which will not be rekindled
By now the noseless fiddler plays.

Just like a foreign tourist peering
At every novelty in reach,
I stood and watched the sleighs careering
And listened to my native speech.

Then fresh against my face, unmeasured
In lawless force, blew happiness,
As if a friend, for ages treasured,
Climbed up the porch, my hand in his.

1929

Rift

1

Not for weeks, not for months have we parted,
But for years. Here at last the day
That the chill of true freedom has started
And the wreath at the temples is grey.

There's an end to betrayals, to treasons,
And no more do you hear, rain or shine,
Irrefutable torrents of reasons
For that rivalless rightness of mine.

1924

2

There called on us of our first days a phantom,
As always happens in the days of rift,
When in its opulence of grey abandon
A silver willow brushed us with its drift.

And to us, righteous, outraged, and bitter,
Who could not lift our eyes up from the floor,
A bird of blessed voice began to twitter
How each had held the other dear before.

1940-44

*

from SEVENTH BOOK

Secrets of the Craft

1. Writing Verse

That's how it goes: a certain kind of languor,
The beat of hours insistent in one's ear;
Far off a thunderstorm's retreating clangor.
Of voices hard to recognize I hear
The pent-up sorrow moan, and plangent lispings,
A secret circle growing less remote,
But from this plumbless depth of sounds and whispers
There rises one all-overmastering note.
All is so stilled by it beyond retrieval,
You hear the forest come in grass new-grown,
You hear the tread of satchel-toting evil.
By now, however, words have come to drone,
Like signal bells the airy rhyming jingles,
And lines, as if dictated, pairs and singles,
Bed in my snowy pages on their own.

1936

2.

I have no earthly use for odic puissance,
Or elegantly elegiac hoax.
To me, verse comes to being as a nuisance,
Not as with other folks.

You just don't realize what gutter catches
Verse tends to feed on, wholly lost to pride,
Like yellow dandelions in backyard patches
Or dusty burdock by a hoarding's side.

An angry cry, the smell of fresh bitumen,
Along some wall a runic lichen sign,
And verses answer, tender, brash, and human,
For your delight and mine.

1940

3. The Muse

I can't stand this Sisyphus chore,
And they call it The Muse, what's more,
"You commune in her arbor deep,"
Also, "lispings divine she delivers,"
While it wrenches me worse than the shivers,
After which, all year long, not a peep.

4. The Poet

Some job, you'll think—not such a dumb thing,
A life with a trouble-free run:
Hear music, pick up from it something
And call it your own in fun.

And somebody's light-hearted scherzo
Do up into stanzas and feet,
And swear that the poor heart hurts so
And moans 'mid the glittering wheat.

Then walk in the wood, overhearing
The firs that look slow of speech,
While smokescreen-like in the clearing
The fog covers all within reach.

Right, left, here a jot, there a tittle,
I dare even draw, as of right,
From devious life just a little,
And all—from the hush of the night.

Komarovo
Summer, 1959

7. Epigram

Could pretty Trixie have composed like Dante,
Or Laura lauded Love's perfervent pain?

I taught girls speech, but Lord of the *quo ante!*
How can I ever shut them up again?

[1960]

10.

Much awaits me yet, I think, and grumbles
At my voice for leaving it unsung:
That which, phraseless, in the thunder rumbles,
Boulders of the nether darkness tumbles,
Hovers dimly, from a fogbank wrung.

I own balances in all the latter,
Drafts on water, flame, and wind, undrawn...
This is why my visions seem to shatter
Such great portals and abruptly scatter
Catapulting past the star of dawn.

1924

*

In Nineteen-Forty

5

One reassurance let me give:
This is the only life I'll live.
Not as a maple, a swallow,
A star, a bank of reeds,
A jet of water beads,
A bell-note in a hollow
Will I disturb your schemes,
Or visit people's dreams
With wan and quenchless sorrow.

1940

*from WIND OF WAR
and
Other Poems*

Death

I

I've been at the edge of something
For which there's no tag, no shelf...
An importunate, drowsy, numb thing,
A sliding away from oneself...

II

I'm one foot up the gangway for some journey
Which all may take, but not at equal cost...
Upon this ship there is a cabin for me,
The wind hangs in the sails—and the dread moment
When my own shore will dwindle and be lost.

1942

*

From **Moon at Zenith**
Sketches for a Narrative Poem about Central Asia

11.

Refectory-like—bench and board of pine,
Huge moon of silver, in the window looming.
We're drinking coffee and the dusky wine,
Imagining some music...never mind...
Above the wall a slender branch is blooming.
There was a sweetness in this, sharp of edge,
Perhaps the sweetness, singular, undying,
The timeless roses have, or raisins drying.
Our land had given us an anchorage.

Tashkent, 1942-44

Betrayal

It wasn't that the looking-glass got broken,
It wasn't that the wind wailed in the flue,
It wasn't that across the thoughts of you
An alien something had already spoken,
That wasn't why, that wasn't why at all
I met him on the threshold from the hall.

1944

*

All souls of those I loved have been translated
To stars on high. None more to lose, and time
To cry; how good that is. The Lord created
The air of Tsarskoe Selo for rhyme.

A silver willow on the bank is bending
To touch the lake's September-bright array.
And wordlessly out of the past ascending,
My shade comes up to meet me on the way.

So many harps are hung upon this willow,
Yet I daresay there still is room for mine.
As for this drizzle, fine and sunny-mellow,
I find glad tidings there and cheer divine.

1944

Cinque

> *Autant que toi sans doute, il te sera fidèle,*
> *Et constant jusques à la mort.*
> Baudelaire

1

Like a cloud-rim's utmost reach
Is how I recall your speech,

And nights more shiningly broke
Than days for you when I spoke.

Cast away from the earth by force,
We were off on our starlike course.

Neither shame nor despair nor guile,
Not a now, nor after, or while.

But alive as you are and true,
You are hearing me call to you.

And the door you were opening then
I'm unable to slam again.

November 26, 1945

*

From **A Garland of Quatrains**

Gold tarnishes in time; steel rusts tomorrow;
Marble decays. To death is all bestirred.
The most unyielding thing on earth is sorrow,
The most enduring, the Almighty's word.

To My Verses

You were a guide as good as ever
A falling star in darkest night,
Untruth you were, and bitter blight,
And consolation—never.

*

And fame came sailing, like a swan
From golden haze unveiled,
While you, love, augured all along
Despair, and never failed.

*

What was mine I have ceased bewailing,
But on earth let me not, if you will,
See the gold-colored brand of failing
On a forehead untroubled still.

1945-1962

*

From **Wildrose Blooming**
From a Burnt Notebook

> And thou art distant in humanity.
> *Keats*

Here, for feast-day hearts and purses,
Let this harsh and arid wind
Bring you but the sweetish smell of hearses,
Aftertaste of burning, and some verses
Written by my hand.

1961

1. Burnt Notebook

By now your favored sister is in clover,
Most winsomely displayed upon a shelf,
While you have nothing but some stardust over,
And coals of fire spread underneath yourself.
How you begged mercy, how you clung to living,
And writhed in terror of the greedy flame!
Till of a sudden all your body quivered,
Your voice as it receded cursed my name.
And, in the depths of lunar pools reflected,
Abruptly all the firs made rustling sound.
Already sacred springtimes, recollected,
About that pyre led the sepulchral round.

1961

*

2. Awake

And time was not, and space was not,
Through a luminous night I made out the lot:
On your table a jonquil, its crystal vase,
The cigar in a whorl of blue,
And that looking-glass which, like a pool's pure glaze
Now was able to mirror you.
And time is not, and space is not...
Even you, though, can't alter my lot.

1946

*

3. Asleep

Black and solid distance from each other
You and I on equal terms must keep.
Cry? Give me your hand and promise rather
You'll be there again to haunt my sleep.
You and I are barred from earthly meeting,
You and I walk grief in grief...why weep?
Just so you will send to me your greeting
At the midnight through the starry deep.

1946

*

13.

And the moon, lurking sly and hoary,
By the gate, looked on as I gave
For one single evening's glory
All my laurels beyond the grave.
They'll forget me. My extravaganzas
The silverfish will eat.
There'll be no Akhmatova stanzas,
And no Akhmatova Street.

1946

*

From **Midnight Verses**

In Lieu of a Dedication

I hide in the wood, go adrift on the swell,
Float on limpid enamel about it,

Separation I'll probably bear fairly well,
But a meeting with you—I doubt it.

Summary, 1963

*

2. First Warning

Why should it concern us, really,
That all turns to dust? We knew:
Where I sang, haven't gulfs yawned sheerly,
Were the mirrors I lived in few?
I'm no dream, nor a comfort, granted,
A benison least of all,
But maybe, more often than wanted,
It happens that you recall
That whisper as verses expire,
The pool of the eye which keeps
That rust-brown crownlet of briars
In silent and troubled deeps.

Moscow
June 6, 1963

*

3. Behind the Looking-Glass

The pretty thing is very young,
But not of our late age engendered,
We can't stay two—that third which entered
Forever made between: among.
You draw her chairs across the floor,
I share my flowers with her unstinting...
Unsure of what our acts are hinting,
We find each step alarms us more.

Like men released from prison cells,
We know some horror of each other,
We're in a ring of Hell's, or rather,
This may not even be ourselves.

Komarovo
July 5, 1963

*

4. Thirteen Lines

At last you spoke the word—and to my ears
Not like that lot... the kneelers-down... you sounded,
But like a captive broken free who bounded
Toward sheltering sacred shades of birch, and peers
Across a rainbow film of tears.
Around you then the silence turned to song,
And through the dusk the purest sunlight glistened,
The world transformed itself for just an instant,
And wine was strangely altered on the tongue.
And even I, who was to be the knife
By which the godly word would meet its slaughter,
Fell reverently still, lest I make shorter,
When I would yet draw out, its blessed life.

Komarovo
August 8-12, 1963

In Lieu of An Afterword

Where dreams are made—for both, of course,
For separate ones they could not swing—
We saw but one dream, yet its force
Was like the coming of the spring.

1965

*

Poet's Death

Now has the voice which has no equal faltered,
Fled is our fellow-dweller of the grove.
To life-sustaining grain-ears he is altered,
Or to that finest rain he sang us of.
And all the wide world's flowers awakened, budding,
To meet this death half-way, and knew rebirth.
But silence struck the planet of a sudden
Which bears the unassuming name of...Earth.

1960

*

Echo

Barred the gates into the past and rusted;
What to me could now the past be for?
What is there but grave slabs, blood-encrusted,
Or the traces of a walled-up door,
Or an echo which has not subsided
Even yet, although I begged so hard...
What befell that echo has betided
Also that which in my heart I guard.

1960

All pledges written in the sand,
A signet taken off my hand,
You left me in the deep...
You found no way to help me then.
Why did you send this night again
Your phantom in my sleep?
All slim and young and gingerhaired,
It was a female fiend,
It breathed of Rome, to Paris snared,
Like wailing-women keened...
Now life was more than he could face
Without me: come arrest, disgrace...

I did without him though.

1960

*

This is not *my* land, yet emotion
Is summoned back by it at will,
Mild is the water of its ocean,
Unsalt, and delicately chill.

The chalk-white bottom-sand caresses,
The air is heady-fresh like wine,
The slanting sunset hour undresses
The rosy bodies of the pine.

Sundown in ether waves suspended
Is of such kind that I lose track
Of whether day or world is ended,
Or my most secret gift is back.

1964

from VERSES, 1907-64

In the Wood

Diamonds four—two pairs of eyes blending,
The owl has two, and two have I,
Dreadful, dread is the story's ending
How my bridegroom came to die.

The grass where I lie is dense and lovely,
My words make a disconnected din,
How gravely the owl peers from above me,
Intently takes it all in.

By spruces we are hemmed in and girded,
Above us the sky, an inky square,
You know, you know it, that he was murdered,
My eldest brother, he slew him there.

It was not done in single combat,
Not in war, in the battle's tide,
But in the wood, on a lonesome log-track,
When love sent him striding to my side.

[1911]

*

Take a look at me. Here, get informed.
Come and see. I'm alive. I am hurting.
These hands that can never be warmed,
These my lips have already said "Curtains!"
Every evening they carry my chair
To the window. The paths come in sight.
Is it you, is it you I must bear
The full grudge of this ultimate blight!
Nothing earthly affrights me or awes
As I blanch here and choke on harsh cries,
Just the nights are my terror, because
In my sleep I encounter your eyes.

1912

I have seen grain by hailstorms leveled
And cattle stricken in the fold.
I have seen clustered grapevines shriveled
And blighted by the early cold.

I saw, like wild imagination,
Steppes blaze at night beyond control...
I do not fear the devastation
That anguish wrought within your soul.

Beggars abound. Then be one—raise
Those eyes which have no tears to give;
And may their lifeless turquoise glaze
Shed of its brightness where I live.

[1913]

*

I won't talk, let out nothing for them to uncover,
But lean from the window in silence, so...
I was led to the altar, too, some time or other,
With whom, I forget. It was...long ago.

I look down from my room on stands of red chimney,
Over each hangs a swirling wisp of smoke.
But I'll close my eyes... And warm lips nimbly
Come brushing my lashes and tenderly stroke.

Not a dream, this, which comforts love's terrors so gently,
Not a wind's little welcoming puff...
He who wounded my soul it is, gazing intently
To make sure it still festers enough.

1913

The evenings feverish, the mornings drooping,
The taste of lips chapped raw, aroma gory.
So this is how it feels, the final stooping,
So this is it, the anteroom of glory.
All day I look through this tight window-socket:
White shines—a little warmer—the enclosure,
Slick goosefoot has the path all sprouted over,
It would be such a joy for me to walk it.
The sand should crackle, and the paws of spruce
Should whip and swoosh, the sere, the full of juice,
And I should see the moon's amorphous shell
Once more reflected in the blue canal.

December, 1913

*

White Night

Skies are white as with a dreadful bleaching,
Earth is lustreless like coke and flint.
Underneath this arid lunar leaching
There is nothing any more to glint.

And a girl's voice, gravelly and brazen,
Does not sing but bawl and bawl.
Poplars, close and black above, are raising
Not the softest leafy sough at all.

When I kissed you then, was this behind it,
This the goal when loving laid me waste,
That at present, calm and weary-minded,
I should recollect you with distaste?

[1914]

Fragment from the narrative poem **Russian Trianon**
Memories of World War I

I

How fond I am of winter's slanting floe,
Its bright, its shadowy, its languid stages,
The rounded fluffy mounds of powdery snow,
The feeling that one won't be home for ages.
A Christmas tree shows blackly far away,
Now caws a crow, the storm has had its day.

II

The fastness Erzerum was seen to crumble,
With blood the Dardanelles engorge their flow.
But in this park they never heard a rumble
Save of a rusty wind-vane's to and fro.
But in the park all is subdued and somber,
The moon is dazzling, diamond-white the snow.

III

Playing a soldier's widow, grief was keening,
A battle-cruiser, like a thoroughbred,
Reared up, and pillars wrought of yeast and lead
The maddened sea churned out and hurled careening
Up to the deathless stars hung overhead,
And no one thought to tally up the dead.

1932

Uncollected Verse

Oh, this was on a bracing day
In Peter's city, town of marvels,
The sunset spread a rug of scarlets,
And deeper grew the shades of grey.

You touched my breast but with the hand
That poets use to touch the strings,
To draw obsequious echoings
To *love's* imperious demand.

You do not need those eyes of mine,
Their constancy, their vatic stares,
But reel in verses, line on line,
Which my proud lips produce for prayers.

1913

*

From *A Wreath to the Dead*

O(sip) M(andelstam)

I bend down on these, as on a chalice
With most cherished mementos abrim—
Of the youth we shared, bloodied with malice,
They bear evidence tender and grim.
That same air—at that brink, thus defenseless—
I too labored to breathe in the night,
Such a night, all of iron and senseless,
Where in vain you would cry out in fright.
Oh! how heady the breath of carnations
Which a dream there once conjured for me,
With Eurydices' wistful gyrations,
With Europa on bull-back at sea.
Here before us our own shades wander,
By Nevá, by Nevá, by Nevá,

Our Nevá laps the sea-steps yonder,
Here's your pass into Evermore.
Here's the latchkey to fit a dwelling
About which now the word is mum...
The dark note of the lyre that goes swelling
On a mead beyond death and falls dumb.

May 10, 1957, Moscow
July 5, 1957, Komarovo

                    *

To the Many

I'm your warm breath, the voice in which you utter,
I am the mirror image of your face.
It makes no sense for useless wings to flutter,
I am with you for good in any case.

That must be why you cherish me so keenly
In my disgrace and my decrepitude;
That's why you rendered up to me serenely
The finest each of your beloved brood;

And that is why you never after bothered
To ask about him by one word or stare,
And in the fumes of adoration smothered
My house, which had been left forever bare.

They say there is no fusion more wholehearted,
That more relentless love than this is not...
As shade from body ever gladly darted,
As flesh craves from the spirit to be parted,
So I am longing now—to be forgot.

1922

Wild honey smells of open space,
Dust—of the sun of spring,
A maiden's lips of meadow-grace,
And gold—of not a thing.

Reseda has a water smell,
Love—that of apple-bud,
But, they have taught us all too well,
It's only blood that smells of blood.

*

And in vain did the Roman regent
Wash his hands before all the people
To the ominous shouts of the rabble,
And the Queen of Scots
In vain from her narrow palms
Wiped the spatters of red
In the sultry gloom of the palace.

Undated

*

So you too have come back to me, renowned,
With dark-green garlanding your temples wound,
All self-possessed and proud and exquisite...
You were in other looks when once I knew you,
Nor did I count on this, the time I drew you
To safety from the blood-soaked mud of it.
I have no mind to share in your success,
Feel at your sight not joy but wretchedness,
And all too well you know why this is so.
But night comes on, the dregs of strength are few.
So rescue me, as once I rescued you,
Let me not sink into the gurgling slough.

Tashkent, 1944

For one lavender May
In my Moscow of the thousand spires
All the star-flocks I'd pay
In their diamond choirs.

[?]

*

The Heiress

> From the lindens of
> Tsarskoe Selo
> *Pushkin*

I should have thought disgrace and fall
Had razed these gutted halls of state.
Who could have told me then that fate
Would make me heiress to it all:
Felitsa, swans, the bridges' lace
And every pseudo-Chinese caper,
Those endless hallways' dwindling taper,
The linden trees' enchanting grace.
And more yet—my own shade I found,
Gnarled out of shape with fear and hurt,
And here this penitential shirt,
And lilac from beyond the mound.

1958

from SAMIZDAT

I

Not to have taken me along
Nor called me love was best, you know.
I changed to destiny and song,
Sheer sleeplessness and swirling snow.
You'd not have known me, to be truthful,
As that suburban train-stop vision
Of an, alas, so fiercely youthful,
So smartly functional Parisian.

Komarovo, 1961 (?)

*

Such as I am. Would that were more appealing,
For your sake. Happiness I've ceased to deal in,
Unlike your charlatan or functioneer,
While you relaxed in Sochi by the sea,
What sort of night came crawling up to me,
What kind of ringing was I made to hear...
  [Not as an armchair traveler invited
   To hear the songs of prison camp recited—
   I got to know them in a different sphere.]

The Asian sky is swathed in springtime hazes,
And tulips, almost fearsome in their blazes,
Have wrought a hundred-mile-long broidered hem.
Oh what to do with nature so intense
And pristine? With such sacred innocence?
These people—what am I to do with them?

To be a looker-on I was not fated,
And somehow I have always penetrated
Into the most forbidden zones of life.
Nurse to sore hearts who ministers and mothers,
Most faithful friend to husbands wed to others,
To some, the unconsoled surviving wife...

Why did you foul my victuals, charging
My drink with bane, my bread with sand?
Why did you have my last free margin
Invested by a robber band?

Because I did not mar with riot
The bitter loss of friend on friend,
Because I had kept faith in quiet
With my unhappy motherland.

Yes—it's the hangman and the gibbet
That set the poet's earthly scene;
We keep our hairshirts on exhibit,
We walk with tapers, and we keen.

1936

*

All went off and departed for good.
Only you, o my last, ever mindful
Of the pledges of love, looked behind you,
But to see all the sky running blood.
Home accursed and my labor blighted,
Yet tenderer song was not;
I stood face cast down, too affrighted
To envisage my hideous lot.
They polluted the language of heaven,
Used the virginal word for a whore,
And in Death Row of Thirty-Seven
Had me scrub at their blood-caked floor.
From the one son I have they rent me,
Flayed my friends in the torture yard;
In an unseen corral they pent me
Of their potently organized guard.
They cried havoc at me and slaughter,
Paying silence in wage's stead,

They brewed me venom for water
And fed me slander for bread.
To the utmost margin they drove me,
And then, somehow, left me there;
Let me be the town madwoman, roving
The quieted lane and square.

*

You won't answer for your tender mercies,
Wring from this what respite you may take.
Might is right. It is your children's curses
That will execrate you for my sake.

*

No lover's lyre to prattle
Enchantment through the land—
It is the leper's rattle
That warbles in my hand.
You'll cry your fill of 'ah' and 'ooh'
At oaths and agony;
I'll teach the "boldest" ones of you
To wince and shy at me.
A lust for gain I never felt
Nor yearned for laurel bloom,
It's thirty years that I have dwelt
Beneath the wing of doom.

*

Like a beast gunned down you will spear me
On the point of a blood-smeared hook,
So shuffling strangers should jeer me,
Assembling in clusters to look,

And they'd write in the worthy papers
That my peerless lute was unstrung,
That my verse once blazed among tapers,
But the hour of thirteen had rung.

*

Some lead off a husband or brother,
It gives me no envious wrench.
Half my life, one way or another,
I have sat on the felon's bench.

Sweet reek of ink from the table,
All jabber and mill about.
This is a Kafkaesque fable
With Chaplin to act it out.

And so in polemical furors
From a nightmare's tenacious embrace,
All three generations of jurors
Ruled "guilty" in my case.

The guards change faces; thrombosis
Knocks out Procurator Seven,
While somewhere high summer engrosses
With bronzing the vastness of heaven.

And a springtime in bud with wonder
Goes drifting along that beach...
That balmy and blessed Somewhere
Is more than my mind can reach.

I'm deafened by raucous cursing,
My parka's all lumps and tears.
Have I been the guiltiest person
On the planet that men call theirs?

*

Why fling at my feet to lure me
Prestige, recognition, a purse,—
When you know, such never will cure me
Of the luminous madness of verse?

Why, is this how offenses win clearance,
Using gold as a nostrum for pains?
I might even give in, for appearance,
I'm the last one to blow out my brains.

Death looms at the threshold grimly
All the same, whether shooed or called,
And behind him the road shows dimly
Along which, deep in blood, I crawled.

And behind that, decades I share not,
Of disgrace, and of grief; and that void
I could sing you about but dare not,
You might burst into tears if I tried.

So good-bye! I don't live in a desert:
I have age-old Rus' and the night.
Try save me from pride, that's my hazard!—
I can cope with the rest all right.

Moscow, 1957 (?)

*

Beneath what rubble-fields my words I breathe,
Cry from beneath what landslide's all-effacement,
With fever heat of unslaked lime I seethe
In a low-vaulted, foully frowsted basement.

Let them pronounce me winter-bare of sound,
Let them clang shut the eternal gates forever,
They'll yet, for all that, hear my voice resound,
Yet, for all that, trust it again as ever.

My head came dearly by its snowy crown,
My cheeks, by burning houses calcined brown,
Are now a swarthy sight which men avoid...
I see the end, though, of my prideful charter,
And as Marina did, that other martyr,
I'll have to down my potion of the void.

You will appear, wrapped in a dusky mantle,
Tall in your hands a ghastly greenish candle,
And with your countenance concealed from sight...
I scarcely shall be very long deciding
Whose hand within the glove of white is hiding,
And who despatched the caller in the night.

Tashkent, 24. vi. 42

*

Glosses to the Poems

Pages 8-9, "In Tsarskoe Selo III": Le Vicomte Evariste-Désiré de Forges Parny (1735-1814), a gifted mock-epic and playfully erotic poet of French neoclassicism, well represented in Pushkin's paternal library, from whom Pushkin as a schoolboy learned much.

Page 33, "Kiev": The visual allusion is to one of Kiev's landmarks, a statue above the Dniepr of Vladimir I, Great Prince of Kiev from 980 to 1015, who was converted before his marriage to the East Roman emperor's sister, and christianized Kievan Russia in 988.

Page 36, "To My Love": The town in stanza two is Tsarskoe Selo.

Pages 41-42, "All has been stripped away...": Written at the time of Akhmatova's separation from Gumilev. She occasionally revisited Sevastopol in the Crimea, which had been a family summering place of the Gorenkos (Anna Andreevna's surname, which she dropped in favor of her Tatar grandmother's, Akhmatova).

Page 67, "That August, like yellow flame...": Carelia is the flat, sandy southernmost region of ethnic Finland north of Leningrad, a land bridge of pine groves, lakes, and Baltic beaches between Russia proper and the Finnish lake plateau. Troitsky Most, or Trinity Bridge, took one of the principal traffic arteries into the center of Moscow.

Pages 68-69, "Phantom": Haiduk is derived from Hungarian *hajduk*. By the late 19th c. it signified a groom in ornate livery standing as an outrider at a rear corner of a noble's or monarch's coach. The spectral tsar is presumably Nikolai II, murdered the year before.

Page 75, "The cathedral doors are flung wide open": Another poem of Kiev. The hetman Mazepa (the subject of historico-literary fantasies by Voltaire, Byron, and Pushkin, among others) was the Ukrainian national leader who attempted to throw off the suzerainty of the Muscovite tsars and with his even more picturesque ally, Charles XII of Sweden, was defeated at Poltava (1709) by Peter I.
The cathedral of St. Sophia (10th-12th ccs.) is the revered mother church of Russian Orthodoxy, with splendid mosaics and frescoes.

Page 87, "This is where Pushkin's exile was begun": The popular wateringplace of Kislovodsk (Sour Springs) in the foothills of the Caucasus was an early way-station on the young Pushkin's leisurely voyage to Kishinev in Bessarabia as a very supernumerary Foreign Office clerk on penal transfer for subversive poetry. Lermontov, another poet of genius fifteen years Pushkin's junior, fell from favor for duelling and for publishing a powerful poem accusing the Court of complicity in Pushkin's death under highly suspicious circumstances. Lermontov was sent into the Caucasus on active service, and his "exile was ended" in Pyatigorsk, where he was killed in another duel. Tamara, in one of Lermontov's celebrated romantic poems in the visionary-operatic vein of Thomas Moore or E. A. Poe, is the mortal maiden beloved of the eponymic "Demon".

Page 96, "The Muse": Sisyphus chore: unending labor; from the legendary King of Corinth who for earthly misdeeds was condemned to Hades to roll a boulder up and incline, which always slipped from his grasp near the top.

Page 96-97: "Epigram": Trixie is for Beatrix or Beatrice, Dante's beloved; Laura inspired Petrarch's (1304-74) celebrated love poems, gathered in his "Canzoniere".

Page 102, "All souls of those I loved...": The occasion here is Akhmatova's return to Tsarskoe Selo, her beloved "toy town", scene of her school days and Pushkin's, from Tashkent in Uzbekistan, where she and many other literati had been evacuated during the siege of Leningrad (1941-44).

Page 103, "Gold tarnished in time...": In a number of privately circulated versions, the first of these quatrains constitutes the last portion of a 15-line poem.

Page 109, "Poet's Death": The poet is Boris Pasternak (1890-1960), Akhmatova's lifelong friend.

Page 120, Fragment from "Russian Trianon", I: The Turkish fortress of Erzerum (Russian Erzurum, Arzrum, etc.) in eastern Anatolia was the object of bitter fighting between Russians and Turks early in World War I, as often before in the history of Tsarist trans-caucasian expansionism.

Pages 123-124, From "A Wreath to the Dead": For Eurydice, consult an account of the Orpheus myth or an opera guide under the entry for Gluck. No philological light can be thrown on her plurality.

Page 158, "I should have thought disgrace and fall": Felitsa was the poet Derzhavin's name for his conspicuously lucky sovereign, Catherine II, in a famous panegyric ode. It is a rudely naturalized Russian feminine for Latin *felix* (fortunate), often used earlier as an epithet *(Arabia felix, Felix Austria,* etc.). The subject here is the poet's return, once again, to Tsarskoe Selo with its vast palace and park, the creation of Catherine II, last described by her gutted and desecrated by the Nazi army in flight. By this time restoration, still incomplete had begun.

Page 131, "Such as I am...": Sochi: a seaside resort on the east coast of the Black Sea.

Page 132, "All went off...": Thirty-seven: the reference is to one of the climactic years of the Stalin terror, 1927-52.

Page 134, "Some lead off a husband...": A *prokuror* (procurator) during Stalin's purges was a quasi-judicial functionary charged with convicting, by Soviet administrative process, citizens selected for liquidation.

REQUIEM

No, not far beneath some foreign sky then,
Not with foreign wings to shelter me,—
I was with my people then, close by them
Where my luckless people chanced to be.

1916

By Way of a Preface

In the terrible years of the Yezhovshchina,* I spent seventeen months in the prison queues in Leningrad. Somehow, one day, someone "identified" me. Then a woman standing behind me, whose lips were blue with cold, and who, naturally enough, had never even heard of my name, emerged from that state of torpor common to us all and, putting her lips close to my ear (there, everyone spoke in whispers), asked me:
—And could you describe *this*?
And I answered her:
—I can.
Then something vaguely like a smile flashed across what once had been her face.

1 April 1957
Leningrad

*

Dedication

Mountains bow beneath that boundless sorrow,
And the mighty river stops its flow.
But those prison bolts are tried and thorough,
And beyond them, every "convict's burrow"
Tells a tale of mortal woe.
Someone, somewhere, feels the cool wind, bracing,
Sees the sun go nestling down to rest—

---

*Roughly, "the reign of Yezhov." Yezhov was head of the Soviet secret police in the late 1930's until he himself became a victim of one of Stalin's purges.

We know nothing, we, together facing
Still the sickening clank of keys, the pacing
Of the sentries with their heavy steps.
We'd rise, as for early Mass, each morning,
Cross the callous city, wend our way,
Meet, more lifeless than the dead, half mourning,
Watch the sun sink, the Neva mist forming,
But with hope still singing far away.
Sentenced...And at once the tears come rolling,
Cut off from the world, quite on her own,
Heart reduced to shreds, and almost falling,
Just as if some lout had sent her sprawling,
Still...She staggers on her way...Alone...
Where are now the friends of my misfortune,
Those that shared my own two years of hell?
What do the Siberian snow-winds caution,
What bodes the moon circle for their fortunes?
Theirs be this, my greeting and farewell.

March, 1940

*

Prelude

It was when no one smiled any longer
Save the dead, who were glad of release.
And when Leningrad dangled, incongruous,
By its prisons—a needless caprice.
And when, out of their minds with sheer suffering,
The long lines of the newly condemned
Heard the engines' shrill whistles go sputtering
A brief song of farewell to their friends.
Stars of death stood above us, and Russia,
In her innocence, twisted in pain
Under blood-spattered boots, and the shudder
Of the Black Marias in their train.

1

It was dawn when they took you. I followed,
As a widow walks after the bier.
By the icons—a candle, burnt hollow;
In the bed-room—the children, in tears.
Your lips—cool from the kiss of the icon,
Still to think—the cold sweat on your brow...
Like the wives of the Streltsy,* now I come
To wail under the Kremlin's gaunt towers.

1935

2

Silent flows the silent Don,
Yellow moon looks quietly on,

Cap askew, looks in the room,
Sees a shadow in the gloom.

Sees this woman, sick, at home,
Sees this woman, all alone,

Husband buried, then to see
Son arrested...Pray for me.

3

No, this is not me, this is somebody else that suffers.
I could never face that, and all that has happened:
Let sackcloth and ashes enshroud it,
And see all the lamps are removed...
     Night.

4

You, my mocking one, pet of society,
And gay sinner of Tsarskoe Selo:

Musketeers, the first regular regiments of the Russian army formed in 1550 by Ivan IV. Following their revolt in 1698, Peter the Great had over one thousand of them executed and their bodies displayed in public.

Had you dreamt, in your sweet notoriety,
Of the future that lay in store—
How you'd stand at the Crosses,* three-hundredth
In the queue, each bleak New Year,
Hug your precious parcel of comforts,
Melt the ice with your hot bright tears.
There the poplar, used to imprisonment,
Sways aloft. Not a sound. But think
Of the numbers rotting there, innocent...

5

For seventeen long months my pleas,
My cries have called you home.
I've begged the hangman on my knees,
My son, my dread, my own.
My mind's mixed up for good, and I'm
No longer even clear
Who's man, who's beast, nor how much time
Before the end draws near.
And only flowers decked with dust,
And censers ringing, footprints thrust
Somewhere-nowhere, afar.
And, staring me straight in the eye
And warning me that death is nigh—
One monumental star.

1939

6

Weeks fly past in light profusion,
How to fathom what's been done:
How those long white nights, dear son,
Watched you in your cell's seclusion.
How once more they watch you there,
Eyes like hawks' that burn right through you,

---

*In the Russian, *Kresty:* a prison on the Vyborg side of Leningrad, so called because of the cross-like plan of the buildings.

Speak to you of death, speak to you
Of the lofty cross you bear.

1939

7

Sentence

And the word in stone has fallen heavy
On my breast, which was alive till now.
Never mind—for, mark you, I was ready,
I shall get along somehow.

So much to be done before tomorrow:
Crush the memory till no thoughts remain,
Carve a heart in stone, immune to sorrow,
Teach myself to face life once again,—

And if not...The rustling heat of summer
Fills my window with its festive tone.
I long since foresensed that there would come a
Sunny day like this—and empty home.

1939, Summer

8

To Death

You'll come in any case—then why not right away?
I'm waiting—life has dragged me under.
I've put the lamp out, left the door to show the way
When you come in your simple wonder.
For that, choose any guise you like: Burst in on me,
A shell with poison-gas container,
Or, bandit with a heavy weight, creep up on me,
Or poison me with typhus vapour.
Or be a fable, known *ad nauseam*
To everyone denounced in error,
So I may see the top of that blue cap,* and scan

---

*The "blue cap" refers to the uniform worn by the secret police (NKVD).

The face of the house-porter, white with terror.
But nothing matters now. The Yenisey swirls by,
The Pole star shines above the torrent.
And the glint of those beloved eyes
Conceals the last, the final horror.

19 August 1939
Fontanny Dom

9

So madness now has wrapped its wings
Round half my soul and plies me, heartless,
With draughts of fiery wine, begins
To lure me towards the vale of darkness.

And I can see that I must now
Concede the victory—as I listen,
The dream that dogged my fevered brow
Already seems an outside vision.

And though I go on bended knee
To plead, implore its intercession,
There's nothing I may take with me,
It countenances no concession:

Nor yet my son's distracted eyes—
The rock-like suffering rooted in them,
The day the storm broke from clear skies,
The hour spent visiting the prison,

Nor yet the kind, cool clasp of hands,
The lime-tree shadows' fitful darting,
The far light call across the land—
The soothing words exchanged on parting.

4 May 1940
Fontanny Dom

10

Crucifixion

> *Weep not for Me, Mother,*
> *that I am in the grave.**

I

The angels hailed that solemn hour and stately,
The heavens dissolved in tongues of fire. And He
Said to the Father: "Why didst Thou forsake Me!"
And to His Mother: "Weep thou not for Me..."

II

Magdalena sobbed, and the disciple,
He whom Jesus loved, stood petrified.
But there, where His Mother stood in silence,
No one durst so much as lift their eyes.

1940-43

*

Epilogue

I

I've learned how faces droop and then grow hollow,
How fear looks out from underneath the lids,
How cheeks, carved out of suffering and of sorrow,
Take on the lines of rough cuneiform scripts.
How heads of curls, but lately black or ashen,
Turn suddenly to silver overnight,
Smiles fade on lips reduced to dread submission,
A hoarse dry laugh stands in for trembling fright.
I pray, not for myself alone, my cry
Goes up for all those with me there—for all,

**Translator's Note:* Here, as elsewhere, I have adhered as closely as possible to Akhmatova's own text which, as quoted by her in this instance in Old Slavonic, represents a slight corruption of part of the ninth *Irmos* (canticle) sung at the Russian Orthodox Matins *(Utrenya)* for Easter Saturday. The sense of the authentic text would be: "Weep not for Me, Mother, when thou lookest in the grave".

In heart of winter, heat-wave of July,
Who stood beneath that blind, deep-crimson wall.

II

The hour of remembrance is with us again.
I see you, I hear you, I feel you as then:

There's one they scarce dragged to the window, and one
Whose days in the land of her forebears are done,

And one tossed her beautiful head back when shown
Her corner, and said: "It's like being back home!"

I'd like to remember each one by her name,
But they took the list, and there's no more remain.

I've worked them a funeral shroud from each word
Of pain that escaped them, and I overheard.

I'll think of them everywhere, always, each one.
I shall not forget them in dark days to come.

And should they once silence my mortified lips,
Let one hundred millions for whom my voice speaks—

Let *them* take my place, and remember each year
Whenever my day of remembrance draws near.

And should they one day, in this country, agree
To raise a memorial somewhere to me,

I'd willingly give my consent to their plan,
But on one condition, which is—that it stand,

Not down by the sea, where I entered this world
(I've cut the last links that once bound us of old),

Nor yet by the tree-stump in old Tsarsky Sad,
Whose shade seeks me still with disconsolate love,

But here, where they let me stand three hundred hours,
And never so much as unbolted the doors.

For even in death I still fear to forget
The grim Black Marias, their thundering tread,

The sickening slam of that loathsome cell-door,
The old woman's howl, like a wounded beast's roar.

And may the snow, melting, well forth clear and strong,
Like tears from my eye-lids, unmoving, like bronze,

And may the lone prison-dove coo from afar,
And boats travel silently down the Neva.

1940, March

A POEM WITHOUT A HERO

translated by

Carl R. Proffer,

with Assya Humesky

> *Deus conservat omnia*
> Motto on the seal of the House of the Fontanka

In Place of a Foreword

> Some are no more, others are distant.

It came to me for the first time in the House on the Fontanka on the night of December 27, 1940, after previously sending a small fragment as a herald that fall.

I did not call for it. I was not even expecting it that cold and dark day during my last Leningrad winter.

Its appearance was preceded by several petty and insignificant facts which I cannot resolve to call events.

That night I wrote two sections of the first part ("1913" and the "Dedication"). In the beginning of January, almost unexpectedly for myself, I wrote "Tails," and in Tashkent (in two sittings)—the "Epilogue," which became the third part of the poem, and I made several basic interpolations in both of the first two parts.

I dedicate this poem to its first listeners—my friends and countrymen who perished in Leningrad during the siege.

I hear their voices and I remember them when I read the poem aloud, and for me this secret chorus has become a permanent justification of the work.

April 8, 1943
Tashkent

First Dedication
December 27, 1940

In memory of Vs. K.

. . . .
... and because I ran out of paper,
I am writing this on your rough draft.
And there, an alien word shows through,
And just *then*, a snowflake on my hand
Melts trustingly, with no reproach.
And the dusky lashes of Antinous
Abruptly rose, and inside—green smoke
And a familiar wind began to blow...
Is it the sea?
    No, only the pine needles
On a grave, the foaming waves
Ever nearer, ever nearer...
     Marche funébre...
        Chopin...

Night
The House on the Fontanka

    *

Second Dedication

O. A. G.-S.

Is it you, Confusion-Psyche,
Fluttering a fan of black and white,
Are you bending down to me;
Do you want to tell me in secret
That Lethe is now behind you,
And you breathe of a different Spring.
No dictation—I can hear it myself:
 A warm shower has shattered on the roof,
  I hear the wispy whisper in the ivy.

Someone tiny, in his intention to live,
    Turned green, got fluffy, tried
        To sparkle in a new cloak tomorrow,
I sleep—
    she alone is over me—
The one people call Spring
I call loneliness.
I sleep—I dream of our youth,
    That cup which passed *him* by;
In walking reality I will, if you wish,
    Give it to you as a momento,
    Like a pure flame in clay
    Or a snowdrop in a grave.

May 25, 1945
The House on the Fontanka

        *

Third and Last

        Once on Christmas Eve...

I'm tired of freezing from fear,
    better I'll call for Bach's Chaconne,
        and a man will enter behind it.
He will not become my dear husband,
    but he and I will deserve such things
        that the Twentieth Century will be embarrassed.
I accidentally took him for the one
    who is offered by the mystery,
        with whom the most bitter times are ordained.
He is late to see me
    in the Fontanka Palace on a foggy night,
        to drink the New Year's wine.
And he will remember Christmas Eve,
    the maple in the window, the wedding candles
        and the mortal flight of the poem...

But he will bring me not the first sprig of lilac,
not a ring, not the sweetness of entreaties—
he will bring me doom.

January 5, 1956 *(Le Jour des Rois)*

*

INTRODUCTION

FROM THE YEAR NINETEEN—FORTY
   AS FROM A TOWER I LOOK OVER ALL,
      AS IF I AM PARTING AGAIN
         WITH WHAT I LONG AGO HAD SAID FAREWELL TO,
         AS IF I HAD CROSSED MYSELF
         AND AM WALKING UNDER DARK VAULTS.

August 25, 1941
Leningrad under siege.

PART ONE

THE YEAR NINETEEN–THIRTEEN

A Petersburg Tale

Chapter One

> New Year's Eve opulently lingers,
> Moist are the stems of New Year's roses.
> *Beads*
>
> We're not to conjure with Tatyana...
>
> In my hot youth—when George the Third was king.
> *Don Juan*

New Year's Eve. The House on the Fontanka. Instead of the one whom the author has been awaiting, the shades of the year nineteen-thirteen come to me as mummers. A white mirrored hall. A lyrical digression—"Guest from the Future." A masquerade. A poet. A phantom.

> I have lit the cherished candles,
> To make the evening shine,
> And with you, who have not come to me,
>   I meet nineteen-forty-one.
>   But...
>   The Lord's power be with us!
>   In crystal drowned the flame
>   "And the wine burns like poison."
> These are bursts of harsh conversation,
>   When all the deliriums are resurrected,
>   And the clock still has not struck...
> My anxiety knows no measure,
>   Like a shade on the threshold
>   I myself guard the final cozy refuge.

And I hear a protracted ring at the door,
  And I feel a clammy cold,
  I turn to stone, I freeze, I burn...
And as if recalling something,
  Turning half-way around,
  I say in a soft voice:
"You've made a mistake: Venice of the Doges—
That's nearby... But today
You will have to leave your masks
  In the hall—and your cloaks, and crowns, and staffs.
Today I've decided to cover you with glory,
  You New Year's madcaps!"
  Here's one as Faust, there's one as Don Juan,
  As Dapertutto, as Jokanaan;
The most modest—as the Northern Glahn,
Or as Dorian the murderer,
And all are whispering to their Dianas
Speeches learned by heart.
  And someone with a timbrel
  Brought a satyr-legged bacchante.
And the walls moved apart for them,
Lights flared on, sirens wailed,
  And the ceiling bulged like a cupola.
It is not that I fear publicity...
What are Hamlet's suspenders to me!
What is the whirlwind of Salome's dance to me,
  What are the footsteps of the Iron Mask to me!
  I myself am more iron than all of them...
And whose turn is it to be frightened,
To flinch, recoil, surrender,
  And pray forgiveness for an ancient sin?..
It's all clear:
            if not to me, to whom then!
Not for them was this supper prepared,
And it's not for them to walk my path with me.
His tail he has hidden under the flaps of his frock...
  How lame and elegant he is...
  However...
I hope you did not dare

To bring the King of Darkness here?..
Whether it is a mask, a skull, or face—
    The expression of malicious pain is one
    That only Goya dared convey.
Everyone's pet and mocker of all—
Next to him the vilest sinner
    Is virtue personified...
If I'm to make merry—then let me make merry!—
But how could it happen
    That of all of them only I am alive?
Tomorrow morning will wake me up,
    And no one will condemn me,
    And the blue outside the window
        Will smile into my face.
But I am terrified: I will enter,
    Without removing my lacy shawl,
    I'll smile to everyone and be silent.
Before the Valley of Jehoshaphat,
    I have no wish to meet again
        Myself as I once was,
            Wearing a necklace of black agates...
            Are not the final deadlines near?..
I have forgotten your lessons,
    Rhetoricians and false prophets,
        But you have not forgotten me.
        As in the past the future ripens,
            So in the future the the past decays—
                Terrible festival of lifeless foliage.

W	*The steps of those who are not here,*
H	*Across the resplendent parquet,*
I	*And the bluish smoke of cigars.*
T	*And all the mirrors reflect*
E	*A man who has not come*
	And could not penetrate this hall.
H	*He's no better than others, nor worse,*
A	*But he breathes not of Lethe's chill,*
L	*And in his hand is warmth.*
L	*Guest from the Future! Can it be*

> *He will really come to me,*
> *Turning from the bridge to the left?*

...Mummers I have feared since childhood,
　For reasons unknown, it always seemed to me
　　That a certain superfluous shade,
Among them "without face or name,"
　Interloped...
　　Let us open the meeting
　　　On this solemn New Year's Day!
This midnight Hoffmanniana
　I will not proclaim all over the world,
　　And I would request others...
　　　　　　　　　Wait,
You seem not to be on the list of guests,
　Among the Cagliostros, magicians, Lyciscas,
　　Dressed like a striped milestone—
Painted motley and coarsley—
　You...
　　are as old as the oak of Mamre,
　　　Ancient interlocutor of the moon.
Feigned moans will not deceive me,
　You write cast-iron laws;
　　Hammurabis, Lycurguses, and Solons
　　　Should take lessons from you.
A creature of peculiar character,
　He does not wait for gout and glory
　　To hastily seat him
　　　In plush anniversary armchairs,
　　　　But bears his triumph
　　　　　Across blossoming heather and desert.
And is guilty of nothing: not of the first thing,
　Nor the second, nor the third...
　　　　　　　　　Sins
　In general do not suit poets.
Dance before the Ark of the Covenant
　Or perish!..But why discuss it! Of this
　　Their poetry told better.
We just dream of a crowing cock,

> Beyond the window smokes the Neva,
> > Unfathomable is the night, and on and on goes
> > > The Petersburg diaboliad...
> Through the slender windows the stars are unseen,
> > Doom lurks here somewhere, it would seem,
> > > But the babble of the masquerade
> > > > Is carefree, frothy, and shameless...
> A cry:
> > "Hero to the center stage!"
> > > Don't worry: now he will
> > > > Certainly take the hulk's place
> > > > > And sing of sacred vengeance...
> Why are you all running away together,
> > As if each had found a fiancée,
> > > Leaving me in the dusk,
> Face to face with the black frame
> > Out of which this hour stares,
> > > An hour becomes a bitter drama,
> > > > And unlamented still.

> *This does not surface all at once,*
> *Like a single musical phrase,*
> *I hear a whisper: "Farewell, It's time!*
> *I am leaving you alive,*
> *But you will be my widow,*
> *You are a dove, a sun, and sister!"*
> *On the landing two contiguous shadows...*
> *Then—the flat steps of the staircase,*
> *A scream: "Don't!" and in the distance*
> *A clear voice:*
> > *"I am ready to die."*

The torches go out, the ceiling descends. The white (mirrored) hall becomes the author's room again. Words out of the darkness:

> There is no death—everyone knows that,
> > It is insipid to repeat;
> > > But what is there—let them tell me that.
> Who's knocking?

Everyone has been admitted.
Is it a guest from inside the mirrors? Or
That which suddenly flashed past the window...
A jest of the new moon,
Or is someone really standing there
Between the stove and chest again?
A pale brow, and eyes agape...
So gravestones are brittle,
So granite is softer than wax...
Drivel, drivel, drivel! —From drivel like this
I will soon grow gray
Or be completely changed.
Why are you beckoning me?
*For one minute of peace
I will give up posthumous peace.*

*

*Across the Landing
(Intermezzo)*

"I assure you that's not new...
You are a child, senor Casanova..."
"On St. Isaac's Square at six o'clock sharp..."
"Somehow we'll manage to get
Through the dark from here to *The Dog.*"
"Where are you going from here?"—
"God knows!"
The Sancho Panzas and Don Quixotes
And, alas, the Lots of Sodom
Sample the fatal juice,
The Aphrodites have risen from the foam,
The Helens shimmered in the glass,
And near moves the hour of madness.
And again from the Fontanka Grotto,
Where love's drowsiness grows cold,
Through spectral gates
Someone, shaggy and red-haired,

   Brought the satyr-legged bacchante.
  Best-dressed and tallest of all,
    Though she cannot see and cannot hear,
     Nor does she curse, or beg, or breathe,
      Is the head of Madame de Lamballe,
  And you, a cut-up beauty,
    Dancing the satyr's tap-dance,
      Again you purr meekly and tenderly:
      "Que me veut mon Prince Carnaval?"

And simultaneously in the depths of the hall, stage, Hell—or on top of Goethe's Brocken, *She* appears (or maybe her shade).

    Like hoovelets click her boots,
     Like cymbals cling her earrings,
      With wicked hornlets in pale locks,
       Intoxicated by a cursed dance,—
  As if off a black-emblazoned vase
    She ran to the azure wave,
      So ostentatiously décolleté.
  And behind her in greatcoat and helmet,
    You who, maskless, passed inside,
      Ivanushka of the ancient fairytale,
       What torments you today?
  How much bitterness in every word,
    How much darkness in your love,
      And why does that rivulet of blood
       Irritate the petal of your cheeks?

       *

Chapter Two

> Or is he whom you see at your knees
> The one who left your thralldom for white death?
> *The Voice of Memory*, 1913

The heroine's bedroom. A wax candle is burning. Over the bed are three portraits of the mistress of the house in her roles. On the right she is the Bacchante, in the center—Psyche, the portrait on the left is in the shadows. To some it seems that this is Columbine, to others Donna Anna (from "The Steps of the Commendatore"). Outside the mansard window slave boys are throwing snowballs. A snowstorm. New Year's Night. Psyche comes to life, steps down from the portrait, and she imagines a voice which is reading:

> The satin coat is parted wide!
> Don't be angry with me, my Dove,
>   For touching this goblet too:
>   I'm punishing myself, not you.
> No matter what, retribution draws near—
>   Do you see—there through the big-flaked blizzard
>   Meyerhold's little slave boys
>   Are kicking up a fuss again.
>   And all around is old "Peter" City,
>   Which chiseled off people's hides
>   (As the people said at the time),—
> In manes, in harness, in carts of flour,
> In tinted tea roses,
> And under the clouds of raven wings.
> But you, our ineffable swan,
> Fly on, smiling fleetingly,
> *Prima* of the Marinsky Theater,
> And a late-arriving snob plies his wit.
> The sound of an orchestra as if from the next world—
> (The shadow of something flashed by somewhere),
> Didn't the chill ripple across the rows of seats
> Like a premonition of the dawn?
> And again that familiar voice

Like an echo of mountain thunder,—
　　Our glory and victory!
It fills the heart with trepidation
　　And sweeps over roadless spaces,
　　　　Across the country which nurtured it.
Branches in blue-white snow...
　　The corridor of the Petrovsky collegia
　　　　Is endless, resonant, and straight
(Anything can happen here,
　　But it will be the stubborn dream
　　　　Of anyone who walks through it today).
The denouement is ridiculously close;
　　From behind the screen Petrushka's mask,
　　　　A coachman's dance around the bonfires,
　　　　　　Over the palace a blackish-yellow standard.
All who are necessary are in their places;
　　The Summer Garden smells of
　　　　Act Five... The phantom of the hell of Tsushima
　　　　　　Is here too. —A drunken sailor sings.
How gaily the sled-runners zing
　　And the goat-fur lap robe drags along...
　　　　Pass by, shades! —He's there alone.
His steely profile is on the wall.
　　Is your Paladin, O beauty,
　　　　Gabriel or Mephistopheles?
The Demon himself with the smile of Tamara,
　　But such charms lie hidden
　　　　In his terrible dusky face:
Flesh which has almost become spirit,
　　And an antique lock of hair over his ear—
　　　　Everything about this visitor is mystery.
Was it he in that overcrowded hall
　　Who sent the black rose in the wine glass,
　　　　Or was all that a dream?..
With lifeless heart and lifeless eyes,
Was it he who met the commendatore,
Having penetrated into that cursed house?
And has it been told in his words
How you were in a new space,

    How you were outside of time—
And in what polar crystals
And in what amber gleamings
    There, at the mouth of the Lethe-Neva.
You descended from the painting,
And the empty frame on the wall
    Will wait for you till dawn.
Thus you're to dance without a partner.
I agree to take on myself
    The role of a fatal chorus.

    On your cheeks there are scarlet spots;
You should return to the canvas,
For tonight is the kind of night
When one must pay one's accounts...
And it is more difficult than death
For me to overcome this benumbing somnolence.

... To Russia you came out of nowhere,
O my flaxen-haired miracle,
    Columbine of the nineteen-tens:
Why do you stare so sadly and sharply,
You actress, you Petersburg doll—
    You are one of my doubles.
To the others this title too
Must be added. O companion of poets,
    I am heir of the fame that was yours.
Here to the music of the marvelous meter
Of the wild Leningrad wind,
    And in the shadow of a sacred cedar,
    I see the dance of courtly bones...
The wedding candles gutter,
Under veils there are kissable shoulders,
    The cathedral resounds: "Come, O Virgin!"
Mountains of Parma voilets in April—
And a rendezvous in the Malta bell-tower,
    Like a curse in your breast.
Is it a vision of the Golden Age,

Or a black crime
    In the menacing chaos of distant days?
At least answer me now. Can it be
That you really did live once,
And tapped the bricks of public squares
With your bedazzling foot?...

A house more motley than a circus wagon,
Amours which are peeling off
    Protect the altar of Venus.
You did not put songbirds in cages,
    You bedecked your bedroom like a gazebo,
        The merry man of Pskov
            Will not recognize his country-girl neighbor.
Concealed in the walls is a crooked stairway,
    And there are saints on the azure walls,
        These riches have half been stolen...
All decked in flowers like Botticelli's "Spring,"
    You received your friends in bed,
        And torment was suffered by dragoon Pierrot,—
Most superstitious of all who have been in love with you
    Is he, with his smile of evening sacrifice;
        You are to him as a magnet to steel.
Turning pale, he watches through his tears
    As others bring you roses,
        He sees his celebrated foe.
I did not see your husband,
    I, pressed close and cold against the glass...
        There it is, the striking of the fortress clock...
Don't be afraid—I don't mark houses with crosses—
    Come boldly out to meet me—
        Your horoscope has long been ready.

*

Chapter Three

> And under the archway on Gallery Street
> *A. Akh.*

> In Petersburg we'll meet again,
> As if we buried the sun there.
> *O.M.*

> It was the last year...
> *M. Lozinsky*

Petersburg, 1913. Lyrical digression: Last Reminiscence of Tsarskoe Selo. The wind grumbles, as if reminiscing, or perhaps prophesying:

>   Christmas was warmed by yuletide fires,
>   And carriages fell off the bridges,
>   And the whole funereal city swam
>   Toward some enigmatic goal,
>   Along the Neva's current or against it—
>   Anything to head away from its graves.
>   On Gallery Street a black archway gaped,
>   A tenor coat-of-arms was singing in the Summer Garden,
>   And a moon of vivid silver
>   Froze over the Silver Age.
>   Because on every road,
>   Because to every threshold
>   A shade was slowly drawing near—
>   The wind was tearing posters from the walls,
>   Smoke was dancing on the roof
>   And the lilac smelled of cemeteries.
>   And cursed by Tsaritsa Avdotya,
>   Dostoevskian and possessed,
>   The City disappeared into its mist.
>   And again it peered out of the darkness—
>   Old Petersburger and drunkard...
>   A drum rolled as if before an execution...
>   And always the incomprehensible rumble lurked
>   In the atmosphere of frozen suffocation,
>   The pre-war, prodigal, menacing air...
>   But then it was hollowly audible,

It scarcely touched one's ears at all,
    And drowned in Nevsky's snowdrifts.
As if in the mirror or a terrible night
Man rages and does not wish
    To recognize himself—
While along the legendary quay
Approached not the calendar,
    But the real Twentieth Century.

But now—homeward as quickly as possible
By way of the Cameron Gallery,
To the icy mysterious garden,
Where the waterfalls are silent,
Where all nine will be glad to see me,
As you were one time glad.
There, beyond the island, there, beyond the garden,
Won't our glances meet again
With the unclouded eyes of youth?
Won't you say to me again
    The word which conquered death
        And the answer to the riddle of my life?

*

Fourth and Last Chapter

> Love passed, and the mortal features
> Became lucid and dear.
> *Vs. K.*

A corner of Mars field. The building built at the beginning of the XIXth century by the brothers Adamini. In 1942 it will suffer a direct hit from a bomb. A huge bonfire is burning. The tolling bell of Our Savior on the Blood Cathedral is heard. On the field, through the snowstorm, the phantom of a palace ball. In the interval between these two sounds Silence herself speaks:

Who froze by the darkened windows,
    On whose heart is the "pale-yellow lock,"
        Who has blackness before his eyes?
"Help, it's still not too late!
    Night, you have never been
        So frosty and alien!"
A wind, full of Baltic salt,
    A dance of snowstorms across Mars field,
        And the clop of invisible hooves...
And there is a measureless anxiety in the one
    Who has only a short time to live,
        Who is just asking God for death,
            And who will be forgotten forever.
He wanders outside the windows at midnight,
    Mercilessly the corner streetlight
        Beams at him a murky ray—
And he finds what he was waiting for. The shapely masker
    On the return "Journey from Damascus"
        Returned home...but not alone!
With her someone "without face or name"...
    Through the slanting flame of the bonfire
        Their unambiguous parting
He spied. —The building collapsed...
    . And in response a rush of sobs:
        "You, my Dove, my sun, my sister!
I will leave you alive,
    But you will be *my* widow,
        And now...
                It's time to say goodbye!"
It smells of perfume on the landing,
    And a dragoon cornet with poetry
        And senseless death in his breast
Will ring, if he is brave enough...
    He will spend his last moment
        In order to glorify you.
                    Look:
He is not in the accursed Mazur swamps,
    He is not on the blue Carpathian heights...
        He is on your threshold!

Across it.
May God forgive you!

How many deaths the poet faced,
The stupid boy: he chose this one—
He could not bear the first affronts,
He did not know whose threshold
He was standing on, and what road
Was opening up before him...

It is I—your olden conscience—
   Who sought out the burned story,
      And on the edge of the windowsill
         In the home of the deceased
           I left it—
                and on tiptoes walked away...

*

AFTERWORD

ALL IS IN ORDER: THERE LIES THE POEM,
AND, AS IS CHARACTERISTIC, IT IS SILENT.
BUT WHAT IF SUDDENLY A THEME BREAKS LOOSE,
KNOCKS ON THE WINDOW WITH ITS FIST;
AND, FROM AFAR, IN ANSWER TO THIS CHALLENGE,
A TERRIBLE SOUND RESOUNDS—
GURGLING, AND MOANING, AND SCREAMING,
AND A VISION OF CROSSED ARMS...

PART TWO

INTERMEZZO

Tails

> My future is my past.
>
> I drink the waters of Lethe.
> My doctor forbade me to be depressed.
> *Pushkin*

Setting: the House on the Fontanka. Time: January 5, 1941. In the window the phantom of a snow-covered maple tree. The hellish harlequinade of the year nineteen-thirteen has just passed, disturbing the silence of the great silent epoch and leaving behind it the kind of disorder which is characteristic of every holiday or funeral procession—the smoke of torches, flowers on the floor, sacred souvenirs lost forever... Wind is howling in the stovepipe, and it is in this howling that one can divine the following stanzas. It is better not to think about what seems to appear in the mirrors.

> ... a jasmine bush
> where Dante walked, and the air is empty.
> *N.K.*

I

My editor was unhappy,
He swore to me he was busy and sick,
Concealed his telephone number,
And grumbled: "There are three themes at once!
When you finish reading,
You don't know who loves whom.

II

Who met whom, or where, or why,
Who perished, and who was left alive,
Or who's the author, and who the hero,—
And what need we have today

Of these ruminations about the poet
And this band of sundry phantoms?"

III

I replied: "There were three of them—
The main one was garbed as a milestone,
But the other was dressed as a demon—
Their poetry insured
That they would reach through centuries...
The third lived only twenty years.

IV

And I felt sorry for him." And out
Fell word after word again,
The music box played loudly,
And over the fractured flagon
In a crooked angry tongue of flame
An enigmatic poison burned.

V

In my dream it kept seeming to me that
I was writing a libretto for someone,
And there was no relief from the music,
And of course a dream is a material thing too,
Soft embalmer, Blue Bird,
Parapet of Castle Elsinore.

VI

Nor was I myself happy
To hear in the distance
The howl of the hellish harlequinade.
I kept hoping that pine needles
Would float past the white hall
Like puffs of smoke in the dusk.

VII

There's no escaping this motley stuff.
Old Cagliostro is fooling around—
That most elegant Satan
Who does not weep for the dead with me,
Who does not know what conscience means,
And why it exists.

VIII

And it does not seem to be
A Roman midnight carnival. The tune of a prayer
Trembles near Empire-style churches.
No one knocks at my door,
Mirrors just dream of mirrors,
Silence is sentinel for silence.

IX

And I have with me my "Seventh,"
Half-dead and mute,
Her mouth is agape in grimace,
Like the mouth of a tragedian's mask,
But it's smeared with black paint
And stuffed with dry earth.

X

. . . .
. . . .
. . . .
And the decades pass:
Wars, deaths, births—
Don't you see, I cannot sing.

XI

. . . .
. . . .
. . . .

. . . .
. . . .
. . . .

XII

. . . .
. . . .
. . . .
. . . .
. . . .
. . . .

XIII

Will I melt in an official hymn?
Give me not, give me not, give me not
A diadem from the brow of a corpse.
Soon I will need a lyre,
But of Sophocles, not of Shakespeare.
Fate stands at the threshold.

XIV

And for me that theme
Was like a crushed crysanthemum
On the floor as a coffin is being carried out.
Between "remember" and "recall," friends,
The distance is like that from Luga
To the country of satin masks.

XV

The devil made me rummage in my trunk...
So how could it transpire
That I am guilty of everything?
I am a most quiet woman, I am simple,
The Wayside Herb, White Flock...
Make excuses...but how, my friends?

XVI

You may be sure of this: there'll be no charges of
plagiarism...
Am I really more guilty than others?
However, I don't care about that,
I agree to failure,
I do not hide my embarrassment...
The box has a triple bottom.

XVII

But I confess that I used
Sympathetic inks,
That I am writing in mirror handwriting,
And there is no other road for me—
I wandered onto this one by a miracle,
And I am in no hurry to part with it.

XVIII

So that emissary from a long-past age,
From El Greco's cherished dream,
Would explain to me without words,
But just with a summer smile,
How I was more forbidden for him
Than all the seven mortal sins.

XIX

And then let the eyes
Of this unknown man from the future age
Stare at me brazenly,
So he can give me the departing shade
An armful of wet lilacs
At the hour when this storm passes.

XX

But the hundred-year-old enchantress
Suddenly awoke and wanted

To have some fun. I have nothing to do with it.
She drops a lace handkerchief,
She seems to blink languidly from behind the lines,
And she entices with a Bryullovian shoulder.

XXI

In every drop I drank her in,
And seized by a devilish black thirst,
I did not know how I was
To rid myself of this possessed one:
I threatened her with the Star Chamber
And drove her to her natal attic—

XXII

Into the darkness, under Manfred's pines,
And to the shore where lifeless Shelley
Lay, looking straight into the sky—
And all the skylarks of all the world
Were cleaving the ethereal abyss,
And Lord George was holding a torch.

XXIII

But she repeated firmly:
"I am not that English lady,
And not at all Clare Gazoul,
I have absolutely no genealogy
Except a sunny and fantastic one,
And July itself brought me here.

XXIV

But I will serve even better
Your ambiguous fame
Which has lain in a ditch for twenty years.
You and I will still have this feast,
And with my royal kiss
I will reward your evil midnight."

January 3-5, 1949
The House on the Fontanka, and in Tashkent, and after.

PART THREE

EPILOGUE

> I love thee, creation of Peter!
> *The Bronze Horseman*

> And the deserts of mute city squares
> Where people were executed til dawn.
> *Annensky*

The white night of June 24, 1942. The city is in ruins. From the Harbor to Smolny everything is flattened and visible. Here and there old fires are burning themselves out. Lindens are blooming and a nightingale is singing in the Sheremetiev Gardens. One third-floor window (in front of which there is an injured maple) is broken out, and beyond it yawns black emptiness.

> Thus 'neath the roof of the House on Fontanka
> Where the evening languor wandered
> With a lamp and ring of keys—
> I hallooed with a distant echo
> Disturbing with my inappropriate laughter
> The impenetrable sleep of things:
> Where, witness of everything on earth,
> At dusk and at dawn,
> The old maple looks into the window.
> And foreseeing our parting,
> It extends its black and withered hand
> To me as if to help.
> The earth rumbled underfoot,
> And O, what a star stared
> Into my still unabandoned house,
> And waited for the password...
> It's somewhere there—near Tobruk,
> It's somewhere here—around the corner.
> You are not the first and not the last
> Dark listener to bright nonsense,
> What kind of revenge do you plan for me?
> You won't drink up, you'll just take a sip

Of this grief from the very depths—
The news of this our parting.
Don't put your hand on my head—
Let time stop forever
On the watch you gave to me.
Misfortune will not pass us by,
And the cuckoo with not cuckoo
In our scorched forests...
But behind the barbed wire,
In the very heart of the dense taiga—
I don't know how many years it's been—
Turned into a handful of prison-camp dust,
Turned into a fairy tale from a true and terrifying tale
My double goes to the interrogation,
And then he goes back from the interrogation;
Two emissaries of the Noseless Wench
Are fated to guard him.
And even from here I can hear—
Isn't this a miracle!—
The sounds of my own voice:
I paid for you
          In cash,
For exactly ten years I walked
          Under threat of a Nagan pistol,
Neither to the left nor the right
          Did I look,
And behind me ill fame
          Rustled.
And without becoming my grave,
You, granite, hellish, beloved,
You grew pale, moribund, and quiet.
Our separation is transient:
I am inseparable from you,
My shadow is on your walls,
My reflection in your canals,
The sound of my footsteps in the Hermitage halls,
Where my friend wandered with me,
And on old Volkov Field
Where I can sob at will

Over the noislessness of fraternal graves.
All that was said in Part One
About love, betrayal, and passion,
Free verse cast from its wings,
And my City stands mended...
Heavy are the gravestones
On your sleepless eyes.
It seemed to me that you were chasing me,
You who stayed there to perish
In the gleam of spires and reflection of waters.
Your desired lovely heralds didn't come...
Only the series of your charmers,
The white nights pass over you.
But the happy words "at home"
Are not known to anyone now,
Everyone is looking in someone else's window.
Some in Tashkent, some in New York,
And the bitter air of exile
Is like a poisoned wine.
All of you could have admired me
When I was saved from the evil pursuit
In the belly of a flying fish,
Soaring over the forests full of the foe,
As *she,* possessed by the devil,
Soared over the Brocken at night...
And already, directly in front of me,
Was the icy, the frozen Kama,
And someone said, "*Quo vadis?*"
But gave me no time to move my lips
Before the mad Urals
Resounded with their tunnels and bridges.
And then the road opened before me
Along which so many had gone away,
Along which they took away my son,
And long was the funeral path
Amid the solemn and crystal
Silence of Siberia.
Seized by mortal terror
From what had turned to dust,

And knowing the time of vengeance,
Her dry eyes lowered,
And wringing her hands, Russia
Went before me to the East.

Finished in Tashkent
August 18, 1942

Carl R. Proffer

A POEM WITHOUT A HERO: NOTES AND COMMENTARY

The English reader will have to accept Akhmatova's mastery of rhythm and rhyme largely on faith, since the translation itself is not a poetic transformation. Akhmatova uses a variety of rhyme schemes and meters (mostly ternary), all of them accepted classical forms, but combined freely and uniquely.

Without some explanation of allusions and background, Akhmatova's poem will seem more opaque than it really is. But if the allusions can be explained with confidence, the different versions of the poem cannot. In addition to the basic texts mentioned below, the Russian reader should compare the early text given in Jeanne van der Eng-Liedmeier and Kees Verheul, eds., in *Tale without a Hero and Twenty-Two Poems by Akhmatova* (The Hague, 1973), which also contains a bibliography. A. Akhmatova, *Izbrannoe* (M. 1974) contains a censored text, but one with a "fuller" ending. An unpublished variant in Nadezhda Mandelstam's hand, with comments by Akhmatova, differs from others, as does a privately taped reading by the poet.

One reasonable school of critics will reject the biographical or "prototypical" criticism found below. It is obvious that Akhmatova's attitude toward her youth and the doomed generation she portrays in *A Poem without a Hero* is ambiguous. Therefore, it is important to know as much as possible about that generation and those personalities, just as one must know such details about Pushkin or Lermontov and their friends if one is to interpret their works and lives as fully and truthfully as a historian should.

The problem of the text of the poem is complicated, perhaps ultimately insoluble. The renowned scholar V. Zhirmunsky had access to Akhmatova's papers (now in the Central Archive in Moscow and the Saltykov-Shchedrin Library in Leningrad) when preparing the edition of her works for the Library of Poets series. Though long ready, this volume has not yet been published, so his solution to the textual problem remains to be seen. Many variants are covered by Gleb Struve and Boris Filippov in: Anna Akhmatova, *Sochineniia* (New York, 1968), II, pp. 357-89. Because Amanda Haight says Akhmatova herself checked over a copy of the MS and pronounced it final (while visiting Oxford), this text was used for the translation [it is printed in the *Slavonic and East European Review*, XLV, 105 (July, 1967), 474-96]. Except for layout, it is basically the same text as that in Struve's edition (pp. 95-133), to which a few concessions are also made in the translation. (Where line numbers are quoted below, they can be checked most easily in the Struve edition.) However, Akhmatova's friends testify that she was somewhat careless about her manuscripts, and that many times the "Poem" possessed her involuntarily after she had pronounced it finished. Furthermore, at least one eminent Akhmatova scholar has privately disputed

Amanda Haight's claim, noting, for example, that "From a Letter to N." (which Miss Haight does not use) is definitely part of the final text (see below) and should be printed with the poem. Another scholar and critic mentions that the use of parentheses for sections interpolated by Akhmatova was abandoned in the final versions (but Miss Haight uses these). [See V. Zhirmunskii, "O tvorchestve Anny Akhmatovoi," *Novyi mir*, No. 6 (1969), p. 250.]

Originally intended for the notes following the text, the following letter written by Akhmatova was also a kind of mystification—a conscious literary device which Akhmatova used to make certain explanations.

FROM A LETTER TO N.

...Knowing the circumstances of my life then you can judge this better than others.

In the fall of 1940 while going through my old papers (which subsequently perished during the siege), I ran across some letters and verses which I had had for a long time, which I had not read before ("The Devil prompted me to rifle through the chest"). They related to the tragic event of 1913 which is told about in *A Poem without a Hero.*

Then I wrote the verse fragment "You came to Russia out of nowhere" in connection with the poem "A Contemporary Woman." Perhaps you even remember my reading both of these poems to you in the House on the Fontanka, in the presence of that ancient Sheremetev maple ("and the witness of everything on earth...").

On the sleepless night of December 26-27 this verse fragment unexpectedly began to grow and be transformed into the first sketch of *A Poem without a Hero*. The history of the subsequent growth of the poem is set forth after a fashion in the mumbling under the title "In Place of a Foreword."

You cannot imagine how many wild, absurd, and ridiculous interpretations this "Petersburg Tale" has engendered.

It was judged most severely by my contemporaries, however strange that may seem, and their indictments were formulated in Tashkent by K., when he said that I was settling some sort of old accounts with an epoch (the 1910s) and people who either were no longer around, or who could not answer me. For those who do not know certain "Petersburg circumstances," the poem will be incomprehensible and uninteresting.

Others, especially women, considered that *A Poem without a Hero* is a betrayal of some sort of former "ideal," and what is even worse, an expose of my old poems in *Beads* which they "love so much."

Thus for the first time in my life, instead of a tide of treacle, I encountered sincere indignation from my readers, and this, of course, inspired me. Then, as every literate person well knows . . . . and I completely stopped writing poetry, and still for fifteen years this poem kept catching me unexpectedly, over and over, like fits of some incurable disease (it could happen anywhere—at concerts to the music, on the street, even in my dreams), and I could not tear loose from it, as I kept adding to and correcting an apparently completed work.

> ("But for me that theme was
> Like a crushed chrysanthemum
> On the floor when they carry out the coffin."
>
> "I drank in every drop,
> And possessed by a demonically
> Black thirst, I did not know how
> To get rid of the devilish thing.")

And it is not surprising that K., as you know, said to me, "Well, you're done for, it will never let you go."

But...I notice that my letter is longer than it should be, and I still have to...

May 27, 1955. Moscow.

TITLE PAGE AND DEDICATIONS

Di rider finirai... "You will stop laughing / Before the dawn." From Mozart's *Don Giovanni*. In Lorenzo da Ponte's libretto the words are addressed to the hero. Further allusions to Don Juan are found in Part I, Chapter 1, line 27; Chapter 2, Argument; Chapter 4, lines 425-27, 437. For the Russian reader these references also have associations with Pushkin's *The Stone Guest* (on which Akhmatova wrote an essay) and Blok's "The Steps of the Commendatore" (1910-12). Meyerhold's production of Molière's *Don Juan* (1910) was also much discussed in those days, along with Blok's play *The Puppet Theater* and A. Schnitzler's *Columbine's Scarf*.

Motto...House on the Fontanka. "God takes care of everything." For several years Akhmatova lived in one of the wings of the "House on the Fontanka" (or "building" as *dom* could be translated). It was the former St. Petersburg palace of the Sheremetevs, built on the Fontanka Canal in mid-18th century.

Some are no more... The line is originally from the Persian poet Saadi. Pushkin uses in it his *Fountain of Bakhchisarai,* but this is from the last stanza of *Eugene Onegin.* Pushkin bids farewell to his poem, and notes that many of his first readers are no longer around—including those hanged and exiled for their part in the Decembrist Uprising. Presumably, the political associations are important.

It came to me... In Russian "It" is the feminine "She" (the word *poema* is feminine). Akhmatova uses this personification of the poem all through her introductory letter.

December 27, 1940. Amanda Haight quotes Nadezhda Mandelstam as saying

Akhmatova changed this date to December 27 when it was learned that Osip Mandelstam probably died December 27, 1938. A few other connections of Akhmatova's poem to Mandelstam are mentioned in N. Mandelstam, *Hope Against Hope* (New York, 1970), pp. 70, 202.

Vs. K. Vsevolod Knyazev, variously referred to as a "dragoon Pierrot" and "Ivanushka of the ancient fairytale," was a cornet with whom Akhmatova was in love. Knyazev was in love with Olga Glebova-Sudeikina (see notes below), and committed suicide after being rejected by her—and seeing her with Alexander Blok. A book of his poetry (*Poems*, St. Petersburg, 1914) was published the year after his death. Akhmatova kept at least one picture of him until her death [it is described in E. Dobin, *Poeziia Anny Akhmatovoi* (L. 1968)].

Antinous. One of Penelope' suitors, killed by Odysseus.

O. A. G.-S. Olga Afanasievna Glebova-Sudeikina was a famous ballet dancer, singer, and actress (the Alexandrinsky Theater), wife of the eminent artist and designer Sergei Sudeikin. She was a good friend of Akhmatova, and at one time in the 1920s they lived in the same apartment [see Iurii Annenkov, *Dnevnik moikh vstrech* (New York, 1967), II, 125-27]. Akhmatova wrote two poems dedicated to Olga: "The Voice of Memory" (in *Beads*, 1913, translated below) and "O. A. G.-S" (*Anno Domini,* 1921). On several occasions they had the same love interest.

In this poem Olga is referred to as Psyche, Columbine, the "satyr-legged bacchante," "friend of poets," "the Dove," "Petersburg doll," and one of Akhmatova's doubles.

She seems to have been a free spirit, but a creature very much of the flesh as well. (The only detailed memoir is an effusive eulogy by A. Lurie in *Vozdushnye puti,* V, 1967, pp. 139-46. This deals also with her later years in emigration.) She was also a close friend of Kuzmin and his set, given to performing in public and private theatricals such as Kuzmin's "Venetian Madness." She was also one of the first actresses to work as a fashion model in Petersburg fashion houses. Balzac's *Splendeurs et misères des courtisans* was one of her favorite novels.

Confusion-Psyche. "*Putanitsa-Psikheia*" was the name of a character in Yury Belyaev's play (of the same title) in which Olga performed. Her husband painted her portrait in this role—and the painting is mentioned in the text of the poem. The *commedia dell'arte* was one of her passions.

Third and Last. The last dedication is to Sir Isaiah Berlin. He is also the "Guest from the Future" in Part I, Chapter 1.

Once on Christmas Eve... The opening line of Vasily Zhukovsky's ballad *Svetlana* (1808-1812). To learn of her lover's fate, Svetlana uses one Russian method of fortune-telling: she sits before a mirror, with a candle burning, at midnight. In the mirror she sees a messenger enter the door; he takes her to her fiancé, who turns out to be dead—at which point she wakes up and the whole vision is said to be only a dream. Her beloved returns the next day, and the moral is we should have faith in Providence. "Unhappiness here is a fickle dream / Happiness is—awakening." The first two lines of the last stanza of *Svetlana* ("Never know these frightful dreams...") were used by Pushkin as the epigraph to Chapter V of *Eugene Onegin;* this ties in with Akhmatova's second epigraph to Chapter 1 here.

Chaconne. A majestic solo piece, theme and thirty-one variations, for violin. It is in the last movement of Bach's *Partita, No. 2,* in D minor.

Maple in the window... The maple tree outside her window at the House on the Fontanka is called the "witness of everything on earth" in the Epilogue.

PART ONE

THE YEAR NINETEEN-THIRTEEN. The last year before World War I and Revolution, the year of Vsevolod Knyazev's suicide.

A Petersburg Tale. This genre indication was used by Pushkin for *The Bronze Horseman,* a romantic narrative poem in which the tragic fate of an individual hero is treated along with historical events—notably the founding of St. Petersburg by Peter the Great

CHAPTER ONE

First epigraph. From "After the wind and frost...", a poem written in January 1914 not long after Knyazev's suicide:

> After the wind and the frost
> I love to warm up by the fire.
> There I failed to keep track of my heart
> And it was stolen from me.
>
> The New Year's holiday moves on luxuriously,
> Moist are the stems of the New Year's roses,
> And in my heart no longer audible
> The quivering of dragonflies.
>
> Oh! It's not hard for me to guess the thief,
> I recognized him by his eyes.
> Only it's so terrible that soon, so soon,
> He will return his booty himself.

Second epigraph. From *Eugene Onegin,* V, X. In stanza ten, Tatyana, like Svetlana in Zhukovsky's poem, wants to conjure up her lover. She goes outside with a mirror, but her lover does not appear in the mirror—only the sad moon trembles in the dark glass. In stanza ten, she has a table set for two (like Svetlana):

> But suddenly Tatyana is afraid...
> And I—at the thought of Svetlana—
> I am afraid; so let it be....
> We're not to conjure with Tatyana.

After this, Tatyana has her famous premonitory dream of Onegin as commander of beasts and murderer of Lensky.

Third epigraph. The quote comes from Byron's *Don Juan,* I, CCXII, and involves a play on a quote from Horace *(calida juventa).* The poet would not have avoided certain literary battles when he was younger:

> I was most ready to return a blow
> And would not brook at all this sort of thing
> In my hot youth—when George the Third was king.

This stanza is part of the long digression on the subject of the poet's youth which ends Canto I. The freshness of youth is gone, beautiful emotions have passed:

> No more—no more—Oh! never more, my heart,
>   Canst thou be my soul world, my universe!
> Once all in all, but now a thing apart,
>   Thou canst not be my blessing or my curse... (CCXV)
>
> My days of love are over... (CCCXVI)
>
>   "Time is, Time was, Time's past:"—a chymic treasure
> Is glittering youth, which I have spent   betimes—
> My heart in passion, and my head on rhymes. (CCXVII)

This is followed by a section on "What is the end of fame?" which concludes poets have a dark future and that "All things that have been born were born to die" (CCXX). It ends with the famous lines sending off his book ("Go, little book, from this my solitude! / I cast thee on the waters") which Pushkin paraphrases in the last stanza of the first chapter of *Eugene Onegin.* The relevance of all these themes (youth, past love, the poet's fame, death) for Akhmatova's poem is clear. The constant return to and resonance of Pushkin is symptomatic.

Argument. The use of a synopsis or "argument" is not typical of the Russian nineteenth-century romantic poem, but rather, echoes Keats, Shelley, and Byron, all of whom are alluded to later. None of the prose introductions or remarks was in the poem originally, but over the years Akhmatova gradually added them.

White mirrored hall... The theme of mirrors is tied to the conjuring suggested in the epigraphs.

Guest from the Future. Sir Isaiah Berlin. Akhmatova returned to Leningrad in May 1944 and first spoke of him to Moscow friends in April 1946, so apparently they met in the winter of 1945.

Masquerade. Lermontov has a romantic drama in verse entitled *Masquerade* (written in 1835), which is perhaps among the works whose associations penetrate *A Poem without a Hero* (Petersburg, the theme of life as masquerade, tragic passion and death).

I have lit...the candles. Byron's *Manfred*, which Akhmatova alludes to later, begins in a Gothic Gallery at midnight: "The lamp must be replenished..." Whereupon seven Spirits come and visit Manfred.

And the wine burns... A quote from "A New Year's Ballad," the last poem in the collection *Anno Domini* (1921). See translation above. The missing person, the one with whom she meets 1941, is presumably Knyazev.

Dapertutto. This was the pseudonym used by Vsevolod Meyerhold in *The Love for Three Oranges,* a theatrical journal (1914-16) in which he propagandized his ideas, strongly influenced by the *commedia dell'arte*. Akhmatova was a contributor to the journal.

Jokanaan. John the Baptist. This probably alludes to the Richard Strauss opera which outraged morals in that generation—Salome's sensual love for John leading to his decapitation and her Dance of Seven Veils before the head—and her execution. Oscar Wilde's play *Salomé* was also part of the "popular" culture of the time.

Northern Glahn. A character in Knut Hamsun's novels *Pan* and *Victoria* (his complete works were published in Russian translation in St. Petersburg in 1910). Hamsun's characters have tortured love relations. In this period of his work love is a fatal battle between the sexes, a source of evil.

Dorian. Dorian Gray. In Wilde's novel, Gray has murdered the painter of his portrait—and in the end murders himself by slashing the picture with the same knife.

Satyr-legged bacchante. Literally, "the goat-legged female" *(kozlonogaia)*. The heroine is called this, partly because she was a dancer. (There is some doubt whether these two lines even belong in the final text.)

Salome's dances. In Michel Fokine's ballet (Glazunov's music) which premiered in Petersburg in 1909, Ida Rubenstein as Salome.

Iron Mask. A mysterious prisoner of Louis XIV, famed from Dumas' romance of that title, and, for educated Russians, from a note by Pushkin on him.

Lace shawl. Akhmatova was famous for wearing shawls, though she objected that in the following poem Blok was inventing things, because of his infatuation with *Carmen* and things Spanish. Thus, in his "To Anna Akhmatova," written December 16, 1913:

> "Your beauty is terrifying," they'll say to you,
> You lazily throw
> The Spanish shawl across your shoulders,
> There's a red rose in your hair.
> "Your beauty is simple," they'll say to you...
> . . . .
> You fall sadly pensive
> And murmur to yourself:
> "I am not terrifying and I am not simple;
> I am not so terrifying as to simply
> kill; I am not so simple
> as not to know that life is terrifying."

Valley of Jehoshaphat. "The presumed place of the Last Judgment." Akhmatova's note.

As in the past the future ripens. See the epigraph to Part II.

Guest from the Future. These lines refer to Sir Isaiah Berlin.

"Without face or name." An allusion to Blok. Akhmatova reportedly said the "rival" who accompanies the heroine home was Blok. And it is known that Sudeikina did once go with Blok.

Cagliostros...Lyciscas. Cagliostro is the first allusion to the poet M. Kuzmin.
In one text Akhmatova's own note says Lycisca was the pseudonym of the Empress Messalina in the Roman dives. Third wife of Emperor Claudius (who had her executed), Messalina was notorious for her promiscuity.

Like a striped milestone. The costume seems to resemble the striped markers used to mark distances on Russian roads.

Oak of Mamre. Presumably this means as old as Genesis and the story of Abraham on the plains of Mamre. However, there was also a famous oak on Chekhov's estate Melikhovo called the "oak of Mamre" (*Mamvriiskii dub*). A picture of him standing under it can be found in his *Complete Collected Works,* volume 15 (Moscow, 1949), p. 400.

Hammurabis, Lycurguses, Solons. King Hammurabi (c. 1955-1913 B.C.), Lycurgus (9th c. B. C.), and Solon (638?-559 B. C.?), one of the Wise Men of Greece, are all famous as lawgivers.

Ark of the Covenant. Apart from Noah's Ark, the Ark of the Covenant was the chest, symbolizing the presence of the Deity, carried by the Israelites during the Exodus, the most sacred object in the temple of Jerusalem.

Face to face with the black frame. Around the picture of Olga as Psyche.

"I am ready to die." Mandelstam's words to Akhmatova in 1937. See. N. Mandelstam, p. 202.

Guest from inside the mirrors. (Gost' zazerkal'nyi.) That is, like the beloved one can see in a mirror when conjuring, as Zhukovsky's Svetlana does and Pushkin's Tatyana tries to do in the moonlight (as here, line 168).

Or is someone really standing... An allusion to the scene where pale, wide-eyed Kirillov kills himself in Dostoevsky's *The Devils.*

St. Isaac's Square. Massive St. Isaac's Cathedral, which stands opposite Falconet's statue of Peter the Great, is one of the landmarks of Petersburg.

The Dog. "The Stray Dog" was a bohemian Petersburg cafe decorated partly by Olga Sudeikina's husband, habituated by most of the major writers and artists of the period (1912-15). Before the Revolution it was renamed the "Cellar of Comedians" (i.e. actors). Akhmatova was a regular visitor; Olga performed there, as did Kuzmin. Blok's diary shows his disapproval of his wife's being there: "Dead people performed there: Kuzmin and Olechka Glebova..." (August 21, 1917). Akhmatova's somewhat decadent poem "*Cabaret artistique*" (1913) was originally entitled "The Stray Dog."

Madame de Lamballe. Maximilian Voloshin's poem "Madame de Lamballe's Head" (1906) made this victim of the guillotine (during the French Revolution) famous in Russia. Note the echo with *Salome.* —The poem is translated in V. Markov (ed.), *Modern Russian Poetry* (Indianapolis, 1967), pp. 499-501.

Ivanushka of the ancient... Here, Knyazev. The allusion is to "Ivanushka the Fool" of many Russian fairytales. He usually has two intelligent brothers who get married and work hard while he lies on the stove and catches flies.

CHAPTER TWO

Epigraph. From Akhmatova's poem, dedicated to Olga, "The Voice of Memory":

> What do you see, staring wanly at the wall,
> At the hour of heaven's latest light?
>
> A seagull on the tablecloth of the water
> Or Florentine gardens?
>
> Or the vast park at Tsarskoe Selo,
> Where anxiety cut across your path?
>
> Or is he whom you see at your knees the one
> Who left your thralldom for white death?
>
> No, I see only the wall—and on it
> The reflections of heaven's dying fires.
>
> June 1913

Columbine. This stock character from the *commedia dell'arte* appears in Blok's play *The Puppet Theater.* Pierrot loves her, but she is portrayed possibly as death (feminine in Russian), and in the end Pierrot (played by Meyerhold) says she is cardboard (as the artificiality of all the characters is intentionally stressed). Olga's husband did the decorations for the first production. —In early drafts Columbine-Olga is called "Traviata."

Donna Anna. Blok's poem "The Steps of the Commendatore" (1910-12), like Pushkin's *The Stone Guest*, is on the Don Juan theme. As Donna Anna sleeps, her features reflected in mirrors, the stone commendatore enters the house at dawn (recall the epigraph to *A Poem without a Hero*):

> It's eerie and cold at the hour of dawn,
> At the hour of dawn—the night is murky,
> Maid of Light! Where are you, Donna Anna?
> Anna! Anna! Silence.

Donna Anna will rise at the mortal hour of Don Juan.

Meyerhold's...slave boys. His 1910 production of Molière's *Don Juan* opened with slave boys *(arapy)* running onto stage, lighting candles, ringing bells dressing the actors, etc. [Yu. Elagin, *Temnyi genii* (New York, 1955), p. 164.] They were also used in his production of Lermontov's *Masquerade*.

Steps down from the portrait. In the production of Belyaev's *Psyche*, Olga did enter the stage from the portrait of her as Psyche.

"Peter" City. Piter was the colloquial name for St. Petersburg, which was built on a swamp at the expense of the common people's hides and lives.

Prima. Anna Pavlova, dying to Saint-Saens *The Swan* (1907). Like the allusions to Chaliapin, Stravinsky's *Petrushka*, old Petersburg, and some of the material on Blok, this was an interpolation in the basic text. According to Zhirmunsky, Akhmatova tended not to cut, but to add lines and make minor revisions in existing ones.

And again that familiar voice. The voice of Fyodor Ivanovich Chaliapin.

The corridor of the Petrovsky Collegia. A corridor some 1500 feet long in the present building of Leningrad University—originally begun by Peter the Great for his twelve ministries (i.e. "colleges").

Petrushka's mask. Stravinsky's ballet *Petrushka* is also based on the Pierrot-Columbine-Harlequin plot.

Black and yellow. The Imperial standard was a black eagle on a saffron-yellow field.

Summer Gardens. Famous Petersburg gardens along the Neva, the city's central park and meeting place for lovers.

Hell of Tsushima. Tsushima was one of the bloodiest battles of the Russo-Japanese War. The Russian fleet was destroyed.

Demon...Tamara. Alludes to the dusky-faced Demon in Lermontov's romantic poem *Demon*. He attempts to find salvation from total negation in pure love for a Circassian maiden named Tamara. She is destroyed by the Demon's kiss, but her soul is taken to Heaven by an angel. It was a popular opera, and

Vrubel's celebrated paintings on the theme were relatively new in 1913. Here the Demon is Blok.

Who sent the black rose. Alludes to Blok's short poem "In the Restaurant" *("V restorane"),* written in 1910. Stanza two has the lines: "I sent you a black rose in a glass / Of Ay as gold as the heavens."
    This allusion was Akhmatova's way of making it clear that Blok is one of the heroes in *A Poem without a Hero.* In Blok's lyric the girl to whom he sends the rose rejects him haughtily, but as she walks out, he sees her face in a mirror and her face tells him to pursue her. It is important that in his poem he casts doubt on the reality of the events, suggesting that the whole thing may be a dream.

Commendatore. This again alludes to the Don Juan theme (Molière, Mozart, Pushkin, Blok), the stone ghost of the commendatore returning to Donna Anna's house to do away with Juan.

You descended from...   Again, Confusion-Psyche (played by Olga) entering the play from the frame of her portrait.

Sacred cedar. A tree in the garden of the "House of Creation" (run by the Union of Soviet Writers)in Komarov.

Malta bell-tower. It was built in 1798-1800 by order of Pavel I in the former palace of the Vorontsovs in Petersburg.

Songbirds in cages. Olga Sudeikina's passion for keeping birds is described in Lurie's memoirs.

Man of Pskov. Akhmatova uses the word *skobar',* noting that it is "an insulting nickname for Pskovians."

Botticelli's "Spring." In Botticelli's painting, queenly, long-limbed Primavera is strewing handfuls of roses gathered from the folds of her dress. Her loose hair, her neck and waist are bound in flowers. The painting also has sexual motifs—Venus in the center, Cupid with a flaming arrow, and Zephyr grabbing Flora, who is clad in a transparent robe.

Dragoon Pierrot. Knyazev again. In Italian comedy and pantomime Pierrot is usually a tall, thin man, his face and hair covered with white powder, clad in a white gown. Gradually Pierrot has become more romantic, an artist lover of fiery emotion who hides his real passions behind a comic mask. —In Blok's *The Puppet Theater,* Pierrot(like the "hero" here) sees another man (Harlequin) kiss his Columbine and take her home—but she turns out to be cardboard.

He sees his celebrated foe.   Alexander Blok.

Don't be afraid...crosses. As crosses on doors saved Catholics from slaughter on St. Bartholomew's Day, 1572.

CHAPTER THREE

First epigraph. With the first word changed to "and," from Akhmatova's "Verses on Petersburg" (1913). The Arch is the one which joins the Senate and Synod buildings. Gallery Street begins there. It was a favorite spot for rendezvous (see Mandelstam's "The Egyptian Stamp").

Second epigraph. The first two lines of a grim lyric by Mandelstam, written on November 25, 1920. The Revolution has come, and the poet stands in the black velvet of the Soviet night, the velvet of universal emptiness. (For a translation see *Russian Literature Triquarterly,* No. 1 [1971], p. 6.)

Third epigraph. That is, 1913 was the last year before the War and the Revolution. The line is apparently taken from an unpublished poem by Mikhail Lozinsky (1886-1953). He is best known now as a translator, but he was an Acmeist, one of the regular members of the Guild of Poets. Akhmatova's memoirs of him can be found in her "Speech on Lozinsky" [Akhmatova, II, 188-91] and her memoirs of Mandelstam [Akhmatova, II, 166-88]. A sympathetic portrait of him as friend of Akhmatova and Mandelstam can be found in Nadezhda Mandelstam's *Hope Against Hope.*

Last Reminiscences in Tsarskoe Selo. This is the title of two famous poems by Pushkin. The later (December 14, 1829) and less chauvinistic is probably the one Akhmatova has in mind. The poet recalls his youth and quick passions, comparing himself to the prodigal son. Russia on the eve of war with Napoleon is also recalled (thus the parallel with Chapter III—Russia on the eve of war again). Tsarskoe Selo is just outside Petersburg.

Tsaritsa Avdotya. Evdokiya Lopukhina, the first wife of Peter the Great (who founded the city of Petersburg); he abandoned her in Moscow and married again.

Dostoevskian. "*Dostoevskii*" is used as an adjective modifying "city," as is "*besnovatyi*" (meaning "devilish" and containing the word "*bes*" from Dostoevsky's novel *Besy (The Devils, The Possessed).*

Real Twentieth Century. From 1914 on.

But now—homeward... The section in italics is addressed to N. V. Nedobrovo, author of a study of Akhmatova which she praised very highly (Akhmatova, II, 328). In *The Noise of Time* Mandelstam describes him as "a mordantly polite Petersburger, loquacious frequenter of the salons of late Symbolism, impenetrable as a young clerk guarding a state secret." [See Clarence Brown (ed.), *The Prose of Osip Mandelstam* (Princeton, 1965), pp. 129-30.] He was also Akhmatova's first love.

Cameron Gallery. This structure is at Tsarskoe Selo.

CHAPTER FOUR

Where all nine... Nine muses. (Akhmatova's note.)

Vs. K. Vsevolod Knyazev.

Mars field. A large open area between the Summer Gardens, the Mikhailovsky Gardens, and the Neva, used for military parades.

Adamini. Akhmatova lived in this building from 1924-1926.

Our Savior on the Blood. A church built on the spot where Tsar Alexander II was assassinated in 1881. It is surrounded on three sides by the Mikhailovsky Gardens.

"Journey from Damascus." As noted by Filippov and Struve: "The Journey from Damascus" was the title of one of the miniature miracle plays put on at "The Stray Dog." Saul meets Christ on the way back from Damascus, and becomes the apostle Paul. Thus the "return" can be either the re-transformation of Paul into Saul, or Olga's (the "mask's") return home from the Stray Dog.

You will be my widow. This appears to be a play on the words of the commendatore to his widow Donna Anna.

PART TWO

TAILS. This is used in the sense "heads and tails" on a coin.

First epigraph. Amanda Haight says that these words of Mary, Queen of Scots, were marked in Akhmatova's manuscript as: "T. S. Eliot." They recall, "Time future is contained in Time past" ("Burnt Norton") and "In my beginning is my end" ("East Coker").

Second epigraph. Klyuev. In Akhmatova's memoirs of Mandelstam she writes: "Osip recited from memory some excerpts from N. Klyuev's poem 'The Blasphemers of Art'—which was the reason for the doom of poor Nikolai Alekseevich. At Varvara Klychkova's I personally saw Klyuev's petition (for mercy, from the camps): 'Condemned for my poem *The Blasphemers of Art* and some insane lines in my rough drafts.' I took two lines from it for my epigraph to my *Tails.*"

I replied: "There were three..." The prototype of the main one is Olga, the demon Blok, the "third" Knyazev.

Soft embalmer. In English in Akhmatova's text. She notes that this is from Keats' sonnet "To Sleep": "O soft embalmer of the still midnight!"

Blue Bird. Maeterlinck's "symbolic" play *L'Oiseau bleu* (1909).

Elsinore. Alludes to *Hamlet*, III, 1 ("To sleep! Perchance to dream...").

Cagliostro. Satanic Cagliostro is Mikhail Kuzmin (1875-1936), poet and prose writer, organizer of "Stray Dog" productions, apologist for homosexuality, theoretician of Acmeism, compiler and entitler of Mandelstam's famous book *Tristia,* author of *The Marvelous Life of Joseph Balsamo, Count Cagliostro* (1919).

The summary of a talk by R. Timenchik at Tartu University suggests that *A Poem without a Hero* may be a polemic with Kuzmin's cycle of poems *Trout Breaks the Ice (Forel' razbivaet led).* Knyazev seems to be the model for Kuzmin's hero, and a few motifs from his poems are echoed in Akhmatova. [*Materialy XXII nauchnoi studencheskoi konferentsii* (Tartu, 1967), pp. 121-23.] See also Akhmatova, II, 604-605.

However, Cagliostro seems not to have been identified as Kuzmin until now. Her description of Cagliostro-Kuzmin suggests he played some role in Knyazev's suicide, or at least that his attitude toward the suicide is one which Akhmatova finds intolerable. Some further information about the prototypes perhaps sheds some light on this matter. In Kuzmin's book *Clay Pigeons (Glinianye golubki,* Berlin, 1923) there are several poems which show one aspect of the decadence of the doomed generation. Three of them are homosexual expressions of love from the poet to another young man—and two of these are dedicated to "V. K." ["The hands I kissed" *("Tselovannye mnoi ruki");* "I'd like to set off around the world" *("Pustit'sia by po belu svetu")*]. Both of these poems were written in 1912, the year before Knyazev's suicide. The first one also has a two-line epigraph taken from the poetry of "V. K." The third poem ("In sad and pale make-up"—"*V grustnom i blednom grime")* is addressed to a "blond Pierrot" whom the poet wishes to kiss endlessly (this poem is dated 1912-13).

My "Seventh." Akhmatova's "seventh book" of poetry included the cycles "In 1940" and "The Secrets of Craft" which were evacuated from Leningrad with her. The book did not appear. (B. Filippov notes that there are seven masked guests in Chapter 1, and Shostakovich's *Seventh Symphony* is alluded to in some versions of the poem. I doubt any of this leads to numerological conclusions. —Akhmatova was evacuated from Leningrad on the same plane as Shostakovich.)

Stanzas X-XII. Akhmatova's note to the missing stanzas reads: "The omitted stanzas are an imitation of Pushkin." See *Eugene Onegin.* "I also humbly admit that there are two omitted stanzas in *Don Juan*" (wrote Pushkin). The few lines which are known to have been in stanzas X-XII (X, 4-6) suggest that Akhmatova, like Pushkin in some cases, omitted the stanzas because of political considerations.

Luga...satin masks. Luga is a town near Petersburg. Akhmatova's note explains that the satin masks come from Venice (like Petersburg a city of canals).

The Wayside Herb...White Flock. Two of Akhmatova's early books of verse.

Triple bottom. The box with the triple bottom has been explained in various ways. Probably the "triplets" which occur in the poem should be considered in whatever interpretation one makes: the triangle of characters based on the Knyazev-Olga-Blok affair; the reflection of Olga as three different characters and the three portraits; the triplicity of Time—past (the year 1913), present (the siege), future (the ending, implicitly looking ahead).

Hundred-year-old enchantress. In one of the variants of the prose "argument" to Part II: "The author speaks of her poem *1913* and many other things, in particular the romantic poem of the beginning of the nineteenth century (the 'century-old charmer'). The author mistakenly supposed that the spirit of this poem came to life in her Petersburg tale." Note that most of the examples given here (especially stanza XXII) are English romantic poems.

I have nothing to do with it. "It" in Russian is the feminine "she" and refers to the "enchantress," the romantic poem which speaks to Akhmatova in XXIII and XXIV.

Bryullovian shoulder. The Russian artist Karl Bryullov (1799-1852). His women's shoulders are round, plump, sloping, and sensual. (In Kuzmin's *Trout Breaks the Ice* he also refers to "Bryullovian beauties.")

Manfred. In Byron's dramatic poem *Manfred* (1817) the hero (who sells himself to the Prince of Darkness) lives in solitude in the Alps. He views the pines from a cliff at the beginning of Scene II.

Shore...Shelley. A reference to Shelley's death—by drowning in the Bay of Lerici.

Skylark. Akhmatova's own note quotes the first three lines of Shelley's "To a Skylark."

George. Byron was present as Shelley's body was burned on the beach.

Gazoul. Alludes to Merimée's hoax, the *Théâtre de Clara Gazoul* (1825).

Your ambiguous fame. That is, Akhmatova's fame had been unacknowledged and her poetry (with few exceptions) unpublished in the Soviet Union between the early twenties and 1941.

PART THREE

First epigraph. A famous line from the "Introduction" to Pushkin's *The Bronze Horseman*. The sonorous ode to the city of Peter's creation which opens the poem is tempered by the tragic story of an individual which follows.

Second epigraph. From Innokenty Annensky's (1859-1909) "Petersburg," a seven-quatrain poem published in *Apollo* in 1910. Annensky was head of the Tsarskoe Selo Lycée and Gumilev's teacher. "Petersburg" condemns the city rather than praising it. The poet says Petersburg gave us only "stones" and the "deserts of mute squares / Where men were executed before dawn." Tsar Peter was unable to trample the snake of evil (which is represented on the Falconet statue called "The Bronze Horseman"). All one is left with is "consciousness of a cursed mistake" and "the poison of fruitless desires." It is translated in Markov, pp. 125-27.

Smolny. The Smolny Monastery and Institute, away from the city center.

Sheremetev Gardens. Outside the Sheremetev Palace, otherwise known as the House on the Fontanka.

And O, what a star. "Mars in the summer of 1941." (Akhmatova's note.)

You are not the first... These lines (19-30) are addressed to Akhmatova's last husband, Vladimir Georgievich Garshin—a pathologist, nephew of the well-known nineteenth-century short story writer.

But behind the barbed wire... Akhmatova's son by Gumilev, Lev Nikolaevich, was arrested and imprisoned in 1935 and 1938. The allusions to barbed wire mean the Siberian prison camps. Akhmatova spent ten years trying to get her son freed; her cycle of poems *Requiem* deals with this.

Noseless Slut. Death.

Hermitage halls. The former Winter Palace, now the Hermitage Museum of Art.

You who remained. Garshin remained in Leningrad.

In the belly of a flying fish. The airplane in which Akhmatova was evacuated.

Kama. A large navigable river which flows south through the middle Urals and empties into the Volga.